Making Meaning:

Seeking the Most Meaningful Life

To Sharon,

Thank you _so_ much for contacting me!

all the best,
"Bob" Lichtenbert
July 22, 2017

Making Meaning:
Seeking the Most
Meaningful Life

Bob Lichtenbert, PhD

To order additional copies of this book, contact:
Xlibris
1-888-795-4274
www.Xlibris.com
Orders@Xlibris.com
718519

ABOUT THE COVER

The serene symbols of the computer graphic on the cover of this book show some of the many rich rewards of making meaning defined as "significant impact":

the trees, stream, waterfall, and azure sky can stand for our high quality relationships to each other which refresh us in our constant seeking meaning in our lives;

the steep hills give us vantage points to view many intangibles that we cannot see or touch but give our lives great heights such as free will, love, and justice. These can give a person much meaning, depth, purpose and solutions to major problems of all types if she knows how to apply them to her daily life;

the bright sun symbolizes the ultimate source of all life, perhaps God, and hence of meaning; and

the geometrical composition of the whole image shows beauty, perhaps the greatest value and meaning.

Not appearing in the cover image are humans. They all have much meaning to other people and things. Also not seen in the cover, the meaninglessness of death lurks all living things, but we can nevertheless make much meaning, especially for others.

(See Section 21, #1 on interpreting artworks to get meaning from them.)

This book is dedicated to

Mary Sands Lichtenbert
(1946–2013),

*dearly beloved wife, giving mother, and great worker
who made this project possible.*

TABLE OF CONTENTS

PART I: **DEVELOPING "MEANING" AS "SOMETHING'S SIGNIFICANT IMPACT"**.. 1

1. IN PRAISE OF MEANING; THE PLAN OF THIS BOOK 2
2. A DEFINITION OF "MEANING" AS
   "SOMETHING'S SIGNIFICANT IMPACT" 6
3. FOUR DESCRIPTIONS OR SENSES OF "MEANING".............9
4. MEANING IS PRIMARILY PRESCRIPTIVE, NOT
   DESCRIPTIVE 12
5. THE INNER CRY FOR MEANING 14
6. THE NEW FIELD OF MEANINGOLOGY 16
7. MEANING AS A LIFE-OR-DEATH QUESTION 18
8. THE COMMON-SENSE APPROACH 20
9. MY START OF MAKING MEANING................................21

PART II: **SOME MAIN SOURCES OF MEANING** 23

10. EIGHT SOURCES OF MEANING.................................24
11. SOURCE OF MEANING #1:
    QUALITY RELATIONSHIPS 25
12. BUBER'S "THOU" AS THE MOST MEANINGFUL
    RELATIONSHIP 27
13. RELATIONSHIPS LACKING MEANING: BUBER'S "IT"......30
14. MY RELATIONSHIPS LACK MEANING................................31
15. SOURCE OF MEANING #2: A SENSE OF COMMUNITY.....33
16. FOUR WAYS TO RESTORE COMMUNITY 35
17. MY SEEKING MEANING IN COMMUNITY............................38
18. SOURCE OF MEANING #3: DIALOGUE 42
19. SOURCE OF MEANING #4: FULFILLING WORK 44
20. MY MAKING MEANING IN WORK................................46
21. SOURCE OF MEANING #5: INTERPRETING ART.............48
22. ARTWORKS EXPRESS
    MEANINGFUL TRUTHS (IDEAS) 54

23. THE MEANING OF ART IS MOSTLY EMOTIONAL.............58
24. MY SEEKING MEANING IN ART: FINDING BEAUTY.........60

PART III: GOD AND MEANING...63

25. SOURCE #6: SEEKING GOD 64
26. AN ARGUMENT FOR GOD'S EXISTENCE FROM
OBJECTIVE MEANING...68
27. THREE MORE ARGUMENTS FOR GOD'S EXISTENCE 70
28. WARNINGS ABOUT THE ARGUMENTS FOR
GOD'S EXISTENCE 76
29. ARGUMENTS AGAINST GOD'S EXISTENCE: THE
PROBLEM OF EVIL 77
30. ARGUMENTS AGAINST GOD II: THE VAST UNIVERSE....79
31. ANSWERING AGNOSTICS 81
32. MY SEEKING GOD...83

PART IV: MATERIALISM AND INTANGIBLES 85

33. SOURCE OF MEANING #7: MATERIAL POSSESSIONS......86
34. CRITICISMS OF MATERIALISM...................................87
35. SOURCE #8: INTANGIBLES, POTENTIALLY THE
BIGGEST..90
36. SIX ARGUMENTS FOR THE EXISTENCE OF
INTANGIBLES...92
37. HOW WE LIVE MOSTLY FOR INTANGIBLES.....................98
38. WE KNOW INTANGIBLE TRUTHS BY INTUITIONS 100
39. MAKING MEANING TESTS AN INTUITION.....................102
40. THE POWER OF INTANGIBLES 103

PART V: MORE ON MAKING MEANING..................................107

41. ESCAPING ESCAPES FROM MEANING.............................108
42. ESCAPING MEANING THROUGH BLIND FAITH
IN GOD.. 111
43. MAKING MORE MEANING 113
44. TIME AND MEANING...115
45. HOW WE MAY NOT BE FREE TO MAKE MEANING........ 118
46. AN ARGUMENT FROM MEANING FOR FREE WILL........120
47. THE LIFESTYLE OF A MAKER OF MEANING 122

**PART VI: MEANING OUGHT TO BE MOSTLY OBJECTIVE,
            NOT SUBJECTIVE** **125**

    48. SUBJECTIVE AND OBJECTIVE MEANING........................126
    49. MEANING AS MOSTLY SUBJECTIVE 129
    50. CRITICISMS THAT MEANING IS MOSTLY SUBJECTIVE... 131
    51. MEANING OUGHT TO BE MOSTLY OBJECTIVE.............133
    52. ARGUMENTS THAT MEANING IS OBJECTIVE.................135

PART VII: CHALLENGES TO MEANING **139**

    53. MEANINGLESSNESS AND HOW TO LESSEN IT..............140
    54. TOTAL MEANINGLESSNESS: NIHILISM 142
    55. REFUTING NIHILISM: MEANING'S PROPER
         PERSPECTIVE IS OUR LIVES...144
    56. EXTREME RELATIVISM: MEANING DEPENDS ON
         A PERSON'S BELIEFS 145
    57. CRITICISMS OF EXTREME RELATIVISM 147
    58. THREE ABSOLUTE ABSOLUTES OF MEANING 149
    59. THE ULTIMATE ABSOLUTE ABSOLUTE:
         MAXIMIZE MEANING..151

PART VIII: THE MEANING OF LIFE **155**

    60. A DEFINITION OF "THE MEANING OF LIFE."...................156
    61. IMPLICIT VERSUS EXPLICIT MEANING 161
    62. THE IMPLIED MEANING OF LIFE TO SOCRATES:
         EXAMINE LIFE 163
    63. THE IMPLIED MEANING OF LIFE TO PLATO:
         KNOWING INTANGIBLE IDEAS...164
    64. THE IMPLIED MEANING OF LIFE TO
         ARISTOTLE: FULFILLMENT, THE GOLDEN
         MEAN AND HAPPINESS 167
    65. THE IMPLIED MEANING OF LIFE IN THE
         MIDDLE AGES: FAITH IN GOD...169
    66. THE IMPLIED MEANING OF LIFE IN THE
         MODERN ERA: MATERIALISM 170
    67. BREAKTHROUGH: FRANKL ON THE SEARCH
         FOR MEANING 172
    68. CRITICISMS OF MAN'S SEARCH FOR MEANING: 174

69. THE CURRENT ERA: MORE BOOKS ON THE
    MEANING OF LIFE 175
70. CONCLUSIONS: BROADENING TRUTHS
    AND MAKING MEANING NOW... 178

PART I

DEVELOPING "MEANING" AS "SOMETHING'S SIGNIFICANT IMPACT"

1

IN PRAISE OF MEANING; THE PLAN OF THIS BOOK

I have intensely sought to make meaning in all its forms most of my life.

I firmly believe that *anyone would live a fuller, richer, deeper and overall better life if she becomes a maker of "meaning"* defined as "someone's or something's significant impact" or its relationship to something else. (See Section 2 on defining this word.) (I have italicized all the sentences that I consider major.)

In this brief book, I will develop the idea of meaning as the guide to make the most of our daily lives. I will make this abstract idea more concrete by relating it to my own life. This will help to personalize the idea. The reader can profit by likewise relating her own life to the developed idea of making meaning in this book.

Meaning has been a major explicit concern to me since that day just after I had been terminated at a major university. *I looked at my newborn son Steven and realized that I most wanted my life to have meaning for him and others for their own sakes.*

Don't you too want to make your life have much meaning? Don't you yearn to live fully and have the greatest meaning that you can? Indeed, doesn't this prospect sound far more fulfilling than just getting through your life with no point or purpose? Isn't something lacking or missing in our lives today? Why not have much to live for? Why not live a life of dcpth? You do not have to go far to find shallow people. They are letting the best that life offers pass them by.

The answers to all these questions are affirmative, especially for the typical person. Reading about meaning can do much to teach a person how to realize the answers to big questions about her life. We all need to realize that humans are basically seekers and makers of meaning, but not in an obvious way.

The life of every person has meaning at least to the extent of her relationships to other people, her parents in particular.

2

Early in my adolescence *I raged internally about my life,* asking such skeptical questions as, "What is worth knowing and doing?" and "Why am I here on earth?" The idea of making meaning finally settled my rages, as I shall explain in this book. I shall also explain here how *meaning is our greatest, broadest, and most helpful idea.*

The *meaning-question asks, "What ought my life be all about?" or "What should I do with my life?"* As William A. Adams writes in *What Does It All Mean?*, page 1, when we ask the question of meaning, "we're looking into the purpose of our own existence, asking, 'Why do I exist?'" Every person ought to give her best answer to the meaning-question, but be willing to revise it if she can think of a better one. As philosopher Friedrich Nietzsche wrote, anyone who has a "why to live" can endure almost any "how."

"What does it mean?" asks the ultimate "Why?" about anything, especially our lives. (See Section 5.) *This is an outstanding question to ask. It should always be answered as directly and specifically as a person can, but it rarely is.* This answer is usually evaded, probably because the speaker does not understand what "meaning" denotes. Nevertheless, *you ought to ask and answer the meaning-question for yourself at least.*

What can be better than *meaningfulness or positive (good) meaning in your life?* What can be worse than *meaninglessness (negative or no) meaning?* I think that "nothing" correctly answers both these questions.

(In this book, words in parentheses define a minor term that they follow except for references to books and cross-references to other sections of this book. Words following an equal sign define an important or major term.)

Very much is at stake in knowing about meaning. Attaining more meaningfulness gives higher quality to one's life overall because it focuses on what matters most, almost by definition, to every person. What can matter more to you than making meaning in your life by definition? (See Section 70 on leaving legacies.)

Meaning is the only great idea that has so far gotten very little attention or development, probably because it is the greatest, broadest, but vaguest one. It ought to have been the first great idea to be developed fully. On the other hand, the idea of the meaning of life which applies to the purpose of one's life as a whole has been developed a little in the twentieth century. (See Part VIII.) *I maintain that the idea of meaning is more fundamental, useful, and revealing than the grand but cumbersome one of the meaning of life. This book will accordingly be about the idea of meaning and how to make it rather than the meaning of life which will be treated in Part VIII.*

Professor Dennis Ford writes that "the question of meaning . . . is one of the last taboos" because it "makes us uncomfortable" (The Search for Meaning, page 15). (See Section 41 on escapes from meaning.) He calls this idea "subversive." It certainly is compared to the current ways of thinking!

Meaning is most real. *Everything has meaning in what* it relates to. (See Sections 2 and 3 on what is meaning.) Which other idea is universal (applies to everything and everyone)?

This idea can ground (give a solid practical basis to) everything. As Naylor, Willimon, and Naylor state in their book, *The Search for Meaning*, page 206, "The search for meaning is a search for grounding." We all ought to think of everything primarily in terms of its meaning as its very grounds.

Meaning is our noblest idea. It regards humans as struggling mightily to find and make as much meaning as they can in the face of their gigantic obstacles such as mass apathy to it and our obscurity in the grand scheme of things. Making meaning is often a noble struggle in which the maker prevails because she is at least aware of the heroic struggle that our lives often are.

Anyone who makes meaning enlarges her soul or self. She becomes righteous in the biblical sense of being in accord with divine laws. Making meaning honors a person: it gives her more dignity and worth. The idea of meaning can best enlighten what we think and do. Knowing about it can add tremendously to one's life overall, as it has for mine in many ways. (See especially Sections 17, 20, 24, and 32 on my own making meaning.)

All this is rather serious. However, I emphasize that *making meaning is the way to get the most joy from one's life because it enables a person to literally get and make the most depth and thus fun out of her life.* It does this by directly focusing on having the deepest impact that a person can. This is often mental or spiritual. For example, as philosopher John Stuart Mill stressed, mental pleasure is always preferred over the physical kind if a person can get it. Making meaning aims directly at raising the quality of a person's life to its highest levels, including joy. I myself have had great joy making meaning in many areas, especially the arts, seeking God and intangibles!

THE PLAN OF THIS BOOK: *Part I of this book starts with how worthwhile is the woefully neglected idea of meaning in enabling us to live the best lives overall. This part will also treat how meaning should be regarded primarily as prescriptions (oughts/ shoulds or ideals, not descriptive facts such as what something does mean to a person) after treating the essential semantic issues in defining and describing such an ambiguous* word as "meaning."

Also in Part I, I will explain how we all cry implicitly for enough meaning. If a person does not get this, she will literally kill herself or lash out in anger.

To conclude Part I, I will treat my common sense (nonscholarly) approach, the new comprehensive field of meaningology or meaning in all branches of study, and what initially motivated my own intense search for meaning.

Part II will treat how the reader can make more meaning from some of its main sources or avenues: (1) high quality relationships, (2) creating a sense of community, (3) talking in dialogue (genuine conversation), (4) doing fulfilling work, and (5) interpreting artworks mostly emotionally but also intellectually. I will briefly indicate my making meaning in each of these sources—not for purposes of bragging.

In Part III, I will examine source (6) God as a possibly huge source of meaning by focusing on the God-question (= whether or not God exists externally to us). Four arguments for and against God's existence will be presented: (1) from the objectivity of meaning, (2) from the need for a creator or greater cause of the universe, (3) from the grand design (plan) of the earth, and (4) mystical (personal) experiences of God.

In Part III, I will explain how the God-question relates primarily to the tremendous potential meaning of the immortal afterlife with one's loved ones offered by the Abrahamic religions of Christianity, Islam and Judaism.

Part III will conclude by summarizing the agnostic's argument that we cannot know whether or not God actually exists as well as the atheist's arguments from the problem of evil and the vastness of the universe.

Part IV will explore the sources of (7) material possessions and (8) intangibles (= nonphysical realities, especially great ideas and deep values). Because the last source is such an important alternative to the others, I will give six arguments for their existence. Important intangible values such as goodness and justice are much missing in current thinking precisely because we do not know what these mean.

In Part V, I will develop various major aspects of making meaning more fully: avoiding escapes from or denials of meaning, especially blind faith in God; making more meaning; time and meaning; how to have the free will to make meaning, and what life-style follows from it. Part V will end with an argument from meaning for free will.

Part VI will argue that meaning ought to be conceived as mostly objective (= existing in reality external to us), not mostly subjective (= existing within in person), as most people regard it today. This issue tells us much about what, where, and how to know what meaning is.

Meeting the major negative challenges to meaning will be the concern of Part VII. These challenges include the following: (1) meaninglessness (no meaning or lack of positive meaning), (2) nihilism (the view that nothing matters eventually), and (3) extreme relativism (the view that the meaning of anything depends on what each person believes that it is).

Finally, I will develop in Part VIII how the idea of the meaning of life emerges from considerations about meaning, especially its sources. A very brief survey of the history of philosophizing about the implied meaning of life in Socrates, Plato, Aristotle up to recent explicit books on the topic will end this book with some conclusions.

I advise the reader not to read any part of this book that she finds too difficult to understand, and instead proceed to read the next part that is not too hard to comprehend.

2

A DEFINITION OF "MEANING" AS "SOMETHING'S SIGNIFICANT IMPACT"

I now come to key sections of defining and describing the horribly vague word "meaning" in general. This will be a Herculean task. I myself have used this word in over eighty senses in the sixty-two issues of my published journal *The Meaning of Life* since January 1988. (All past issues are available by contacting *seekerofmeaning@yahoo.com.*) This journal was featured in *The Chicago Tribune on December 3, 1991.* Over 3,400 people subscribed to it as a result of this feature finely written by journalist Jon Anderson and reprinted as the last essay in his book, *City Watch.* I feel greatly gratified that many readers of my journal told me that it made more meaning for them.

The *etymology* (the origination of a word) of "meaning" goes back to the thirteenth century from an Old English word for "signify to a person." This word started as highly subjective (= wholly inside or within a person's awareness only, and see Section 48 for a fuller description.) "Meaning" was not used much until the middle of the twentieth century in Europe. This word thus could not be used by such great thinkers as Plato, Aristotle, Aquinas, and Kant, although all major philosophers can be interpreted to have treated it in an implied way. (See Section 61.)

I need to define "meaning" at the very start, as everyone should do as soon as they introduce any ambiguous or unfamiliar word. (See Appendix I on definitions.) After giving much thought and—mostly!—agony to this definition, I decided that *the following best obeys all the laws of logic for defining a term: "meaning" is (=) something's significant impact." In other words, "meaning" refers to the major effects that anything has.* How anything relates to something else is what it "means" in general.

This definition refers to "things," but in most of this book it will apply to humans or "someone's" impact or effect on other people.

Since a thing usually has many impacts or effects, its total meaning consists of the total of all these. However, there are too many impacts for us to know completely and conveniently except for simple things. One's society must select what is the "significant" or main impact of anything *by its consensus and then by its definition in a dictionary* according to the the common usage of the word by most people in the society. *This usage ought to be respected to communicate clearly about the meaning of anything unless a word is used in one of its special senses.* (I will further describe "significant impact" in Section 3.)

The emphasis on impacts, effects or relationships of this definition demonstrates that meaning is mostly objective, not subjective. Impacts are physical effects that can be observed: they clearly come from things external to us. "Meaning should not be conceived of as subjective because this represents only what a person believes which can be entirely incorrect. Professor Manuel Velasquez asks in his textbook, *Philosophy* (2014 edition), page 629, is it meaningful to make piles of sand on a beach? One can change this to mud. (See Section 48.) He states that to get meaning we ought to "connect with something bigger or more important than ourselves," for examples, God, a social cause, family and other people in general. Similarly, architect Maya Lin writes that, "We are connected to one another through time by our creations, works, images, thoughts, and writings," *The Meaning of Life*, edited by Richard Kinnier et al., page 188.

The many rich senses of "meaning" make it extremely ambiguous (a word with more than one sense or usage). Examples of some of the senses in which I myself have used "meaning" include "success, love, real, precious," and at least seventy-six other senses.

So much ambiguity seems to prohibit the use of "meaning," but this use can be allowed by a law of the logic of language. (See Appendix I.) This law commands us to *specify the precise sense in which "meaning" is used every time that it is not used in the sense of its definition as "significant impact." I will do this in parentheses in this book,* as awkward as "meaning (in the sense of '_____')" sounds. I need to forbear this ineloquent expression so that I can communicate in a precise way the extremely ambiguous term "meaning" each time that it is used in one of its special senses, not its definition.

(I learned this law of logic, and many others, for dealing with ambiguous words from doing research for my PhD dissertation from Tulane University in New Orleans on the legendary teacher of philosophers, Morris R. Cohen. His 1934 textbook on logic, *An Introduction to Logic and Scientific Method,* was the most widely used during his era. It remains, in my estimation, the most helpful text for learning how to think logically. *The laws of logic provide objective tests of the soundness of all* rational thinking.(See Appendix I on arguments and Section 49 on the objectivity of logic.)

The word "meaning" has another tricky aspect in that it often suggests a good connotation (strongly suggested emotional sense) since it frequently refers to what is favorable or positive in some way. For example, a person's house generally has "meaning" to her in that it is her most prized possession, biggest investment, place of many memories, and source of shelter—all these meanings are positive (good). *Since using the neutral term "meaning" for the positive term "meaningful" is common usage, I will not indicate it in parentheses whenever it is clear from its context that I am using either of these two words in the sense of a "good (positive) impact."* In other words, I will call anything that has good impact overall either to "have meaning" or "to be meaningful" without using parentheses following it specifying the special sense in which it is used.

Since the word "meaning" can have so many senses or references, it is rarely fitting to talk about "the meaning" of anything, for example, "the meaning of Christmas." "A meaning" or just "meaning" specifying its reference is usually more appropriate, for example, "Christmas has special meaning for the children who get presents then," not "The meaning of Christmas to children is mostly getting presents."

We need now a new way of talking about "meaning, for example, "meaningless" should refer to "lacking meaning," not "no meaning." (See Section 53 on the two types of meaninglessness.) I hope that it is not too late to overcome the current extremely subjective or personal conception and language of meaning. (See Part VI, especially Section 48.)

3

FOUR DESCRIPTIONS OR
SENSES OF "MEANING"

To further elucidate the highly ambiguous word "meaning," I will next briefly describe four of its main senses or usages. *I have selected these four senses because they are the most common usages of "meaning."* My hope is that these four senses will help to clarify what "meaning" designates in general. All four senses are not implied every time that this word is used, but they should give the reader a better grasp of this highly ambiguous word.

A. "IMPACT" makes up the genus (the general class that every member of a term needs to have, according to Aristotle's laws of logic—see Appendix I) in the definition of *"meaning." This word generally designates the effect that anything has on something. "Meaning" also designates the consequences that result from the power or force of anything on something else.*

I conceive of "impact" not so much as a "collision" or "forceful contact" as "the main effect of anything in relation to something else." Since a thing's meaning consists of its primary or most important aspects (See Section 2.), I think that the strong word "impact" is justified as its genus. How a thing impinges on other things is its meaning.

This first sense of "meaning" tells us the change, including mental, that results in anything after it is impacted or comes into contact with something. "Impact" often denotes "a forceful collision" between two things, but this is often not so strong for "meaning;" for example, "impact" in regard to the effect of an idea is closer to the gentler sense of an "influence" on one's thinking rather than a "forceful collision" on it.

Meaning as "impact" accords well with the emphasis on acting on what is thought to be meaningful instead of just thinking about it. This is especially true for implementing one's conception of the meaning of life. (See Section 60.)

B. "SIGNIFICANT" makes up the specific difference (the unique trait that distinguishes a thing from others in its genus or general class, again according to Aristotle on laws for defining terms) of the definition of "meaning." *"Significance" designates what is "important" about anything to us or a person. It is whatever is most worthy of attention. So whenever we talk about the "meaning" of anything, we also are talking about why it matters to us along with its impact. It is what we care about.* Very hopefully, this will be something that is worthwhile or valuable in itself, but this is quite hard to specify (Harry Frankfurt, *The Importance of What We Care For, page 94*).

"Significance" can be either objective or subjective, whereas "*important*" *is often subjective* in that it varies much from person to person. *Perhaps a more neutral term is "special,"* for example, a person's deepest positive quality such as generosity or integrity is often considered special.

C. "PURPOSE" *best suits the grand "meaning of life"* rather than the "meaning" of something. The meaning of life is the main purpose (goal or aim) of one's life, for examples, working at a fulfilling job, raising children, dedicating to a social cause such as liberating oppressed people and animals, donating to charities, and committing to God.

We often designate the goal of any action as its "purpose." A purpose moves a person to act. It is one's intention, but it can be a small one or a project for the rest of one's life. Such purposes are uniquely human. The sciences no longer hold that anything has a purpose other than the subjective ones that humans give it. (See Section 27, #2 for an exception that criticizes this view.)

D. "VALUES," especially the good (= those actions that we ought to prefer or approve of), have much meaning. As philosopher John Dewey put it in his colloquial writing style, values are what we "prize" or "cherish." They do not need to be the great or deep ones such as truth, beauty, justice, and the holy to be meaningful to us. They can include even money, which has value and hence meaning to everyone. (See Sections 33 and 34 on materialism.) However, prescriptive values such as goodness and justice have the potential to be most meaningful, if you can comprehend or somehow "sink your teeth into" one. These values exist as intangibles. (See Sections 35 and 36 on intangibles and arguments for them.)

Meaning is the greatest value because it encompasses all others. All values obviously have meaning, but not vice versa, for example, goodness has meaning, but not all meaning is goodness and so on for all the other great values. They are thereby subsets of meaning.

Meaning is like the mother who gave birth to all values (see implications in Section 26), just as philosophy did for all fields of study. Perhaps this is the reason that meaning is the last great idea to be developed. Perhaps also we could clarify the deep values that have eluded us for centuries if we develop the idea of meaning to do this, but such clarifying would be too big a task for this book with its common sense approach. (See Section 8.)

Disvalues such as evil also can have much meaning to us, but in its negative sense of "meaninglessness" (in the sense of "their lacking positive meaning)" These are to be minimized as much as we can, of course, but they cannot be totally eliminated, for example, death. (See Section 52 on meaninglessness.)

Impact, significance, purpose and values—these are the four main senses in which the word "meaning" is most frequently used. They describe what "meaning" often refers to in general. *Try to keep the four senses in mind whenever you think about "meaning,"* but remember that none of them is necessarily implied in any use of this word. I hope that the definition of "meaning" as "something's significant impact" and these four descriptions have clarified this highly ambiguous word at the start of this book.

I will not be concerned with the topic of the meaning of words and symbols. This is the one area of meaning that has already been developed by many philosophers and linguists, although they have hardly clarified it or enlightened us. *It is now time to make meaning in our lives, not just in words.* Human lives are surely larger, more fitting and appropriate targets for meaning than words. (See Section 70 for more on applying meaning to our lives.)

4

MEANING IS PRIMARILY PRESCRIPTIVE, NOT DESCRIPTIVE

I emphasize that *meaning is far more than factual: it is mostly philosophical. Like philosophy (= basic beliefs about deep values and knowing reality), meaning is prescriptive (=) states what should ought to be rather than what should is and exists which is descriptive. Prescriptions give us ideals that we ought to live by and standards to judge by.* These cannot come from the physical world: they are *intangibles (= nonphysical realities—see Sections 35-40) existing in their own immaterial realm.*

Intangibles consist of our greatest values (such as truth, goodness, justice, and beauty) and greatest ideas (such as the self, free will, and love). Most of these are both, for examples, all these values are ideas which can be embodied on earth in us.

Whenever we think about meaning in factual terms, we are using "meaning" in its descriptive sense. On the other hand, whenever we talk about how we ought to think deep values such as goodness and justice we are using "meaning" in its prescriptive sense. This is a huge difference that we all need to attend to carefully. Since meaning is mostly a philosophical concept, its primary helpfulness by far is its prescriptive sense. (See Part VI on the subjective and objective meaning.)

Whether or not a prescriptive level or realm of reality exists beyond the descriptive or physical asks perhaps the most basic question of philosophy. I will argue that a prescriptive level of guiding deep values and ideas such as goodness and justice exists in Sections 26-27 on four arguments for God's existence, Section 36 on six arguments for intangibles or nonphysical realities (explained in Section 35) and Sections 38-40 on how we can know these by testable intuitions.

What is most distinctive about philosophy, including meaning, is that it studies intangibles and prescriptions. Without these, there would be no philosophy. We would be left with just facts, ideas abstracted from them, and unprovable opinions. It is quite hard to know prescriptions and intangibles, of course, but we can know them to some extent in the traditional way of thinking hard in general using the laws of logic. (See Appendix I and Section 38 on knowing intangibles.)

Prescriptions give us a higher level of reality than the physical one. In our super-scientific age, we sorely need more meaning to believe in than the physical, but only if this can be demonstrated to exist by strong arguments which I will give chiefly in Section 36.

Meaning, like all other prescriptions, are what is called in a derogatory sense mere "opinions." Yet, we must never forget that *some opinions can be proven by logic to express more truth than others.* (See Section 70 on broadening truth.)

Like philosophy and meaning, *logic as their methodological branch is prescriptive because it teaches us laws on how we ought to think. It gives us objective standards to judge all thinking.* (See Section 52, #2.) *Logic is much needed, but little known today. I propose that everyone take at least a cursory course on logic to improve their thinking.* Then they would know at least what constitutes logical thinking and how to go about it.

Making Meaning is a book of philosophy of daily life, not the tedious and irrelevant academic philosophy with hundreds of intimidating footnotes. Every person has a philosophy: the only alternatives are to have a good (developed) guiding philosophy or a weak one. The word "philosophy" comes from ancient Greek for "the love of wisdom." Most philosophers have long since abandoned this goal except perhaps for each person. I maintain that the true goal of philosophy is making meaning. Loving to do this is wisdom, from the point of view of meaning. Perhaps applying the developed idea of making meaning can free philosophy from the almost total uselessness and irrelevance that it has had for many years. Traditional philosophy has failed us in major ways by not focusing on meaning.

This book contains some implied popular, really populist, psychologies about living an enriched life. It can also be classified as "self-help," but philosophy of daily life is harder and more rigorous than this. Also, this book's emphasis on prescriptions (shoulds or oughts and values) differs much from the self-help's limitations to the descriptive or factual realm.

5

THE INNER CRY FOR MEANING

Everyone cries out at least to themselves for meaning in their lives. We all want our lives to measure up to our own standards of meaning. Who does not want to be missed when they are dead or what we euphemistically call "passed"? However, famed psychologist Sigmund Freud disagreed strongly that the cry for meaning is normal or healthy (Gerhard Sauter, *The Quest for Meaning, page 85). Freud* wrote that, "The moment that one searches for meaning and value, one is sick because neither exists in an objective way; one only has to acknowledge that one has a quantity of libido" (sex drive), (quoted by Wessel Stocker, "*Is the Quest for Meaning the Quest for God?*" page 99. Nevertheless, to cry out for meaning is clearly vital and healthy for anyone because it shows love of and curiosity about one's life. The cry for meaning rarely signifies that we are desperate for it. Insufficient sex is only a non-essential tone in the cry for meaning.

While we rarely cry "Meaning!" aloud or explicitly, *we all do cry internally that our lives mean something or matter,* at least to ourselves and in our relationships. Hearing one's inner voice in the omnipresent hubbub in current society requires much effort and a strong sense of self.

One's cries vary in intensity. Often they sound like the biblical "still small voice" that Elijah heard, although they clearly are not the voice of God speaking to a person. We tend to cry loudly, sometimes boisterously, for meaning only in times of a personal crisis or extreme stress. A life in which the inner cry for meaning has been silenced too much cannot be endured because it expresses needs at the very depths of a person.

A person needs to soothe the cry by making as much of the missing meaning as she can, usually from the sources of meaning that she lacks. (See Section 43 on making more meaning.) This is rarely easy to do. Like meaning in general, the cry for it is tricky, but it plays a basic role in our lives.

We all have an inner voice and ears to hear it, but few of us recognize or fathom them. This voice is more than one's conscience (a person's inner sense of right or wrong—Socrates placed so much confidence in the silence of his conscience at his trial that he did not oppose his execution.) *Because the inner cry for meaning demands much hard thinking, effort and work, many people suppress it by pursuing escapes. (See Sections 41 and 42.)*

The inner voice consists of thinking going on inside a person's mind, but not her brain. Only the person herself can say and hear it: we have no "ears" to hear the inner voice, nor vocal chords to express it. This is this incredible and most amazing. *What wonderful and mysterious beings we are!*

I contend in this book that the idea of meaning can best help us understand such mysteries in humans (and the multitude of them now in the universe—see Section 36, #1). We are, at our core, makers of meaning, but not in a simple way. There are no easy answers to life's big question. Humans are (descriptive) and ought (prescriptive) to be essentially meaning makers.

6

THE NEW FIELD OF
MEANINGOLOGY

In this book I will develop for the first time ever the *new field of meaningology* (= the study of meaning). Philosopher Michael Polanyi mentioned "meaning" only a few times in his final (actually posthumous or after his death) book titled *Meaning (1975)*. Likewise, Ernest Becker's *Birth and Death of Meaning (second edition, 1971)* uses this idea in its very title, but then in a very minor way near the end of his book itself. He and Polanyi apparently recognized the importance of meaning, but they did not directly develop this idea and its issues. Neither did the Dalai Lama, even though an English translation of some of his writings on the main teachings of Tibetan Buddhism was published as *The Meaning of Life (1992)*.

I will in this book develop only the idea of meaning itself, but not how it applies to other fields of study such as music, literature, biology, and sociology. *Meaningology would treat all fields in terms of what each field ought to mean.* Wouldn't this be more enlightening by far than the descriptive way in which these fields have been studied in the past? (See Section 4 on the difference between the prescriptive ought and the descriptive is.) I will not make these applications in this book because that would be too long and they would require much knowledge about every field to determine the main meanings in each. *The idea of meaning promises to be a highly fertile way to approach all knowledge.*

Meaningology studies meaning as the basic or fundamental idea that ought to guide all our thinking and living. The fact that so far it has explicitly—see Section 61—not done this at all implies that *all past thinking is misguided* because it does not stem from a developed conception of the meaning of anything. Perhaps this is the reason that traditional philosophy has had so little effect on our work-a-day lives. I maintain that *applying the idea of meaning would beneficially revolutionize all our thinking and acting* by putting both of them in its vital perspective. Nobel

Prize–winning physicist Richard Feynman asserted that if we find meaning in our lives, "then great human forces would be unleashed" *(The Meaning of It All, page 32). To approach something in terms of its meaning thinks in a new way.* Philosopher Suzanne Langer has written that the ability of an age to understand its experiences depends not only on the events of its time, but in the concepts at its disposal, *Philosophy in a New Key*, 1951 edition, page 17. "Meaning" certainly qualifies as one of these innovative concepts for our age.

Ideas are abstract and general whereas our lives are concrete and particular. These two obviously do not match each other well. The result is that ideas lose the very sense of life, as philosophers Henri Bergson and Jerome Bruner in his *Acts of Meaning* repeatedly warned us. As spiritual teacher Eckhart Tolle writes, "Words . . . only covered up the mystery with a label." (*A New Earth: Awakening to Your Life's Purpose, page 25*). However, the idea of meaning, since it vitally concerns what anything signifies and how it affects relates to us (see Sections 2 and 3), applies well to actual existence and our experience.

Albert Camus

7

MEANING AS A LIFE-OR-DEATH QUESTION

A person's life must mean enough to her to even want to continue living. Writer Albert Camus in his *Myth of Sisyphus* wrote that *if a person's life lacks meaning too much to her, she will commit suicide:* "There is but one truly philosophical problem and that is suicide. Judging whether or not life is worth living amounts to answering the fundamental question of philosophy. All the rest . . . are [mental] games. . . . the meaning of life is the most urgent of questions." Camus thus thought that philosophy's basic task is to attain at least enough meaning to sustain a person in continuing to live her life. He wrote how we can do much more than this in his rather surrealistic (strange and unrealistic) novels.

I believe that Camus is totally correct to insist that the fundamental question of philosophy ought to be about living a worthwhile or meaningful life and that any person whose life does not make enough meaning for her will commit suicide. *Thus, the fundamental question of all our lives centers on making meaning, although few of us use this term explicitly. (See Sections 41 and 61.)* With this book I want to make this making more explicit and hence fuller in our lives.

We will read in Section 62 how *Socrates preferred his own death to not being allowed to ask questions about fundamental ideas and values. His life offers us a dramatic ideal of commitment to making meaning.*

Also, if a person's life lacks meaning too much for her, for examples, hostile parents and extreme poverty, *she may commit violence because she will be quite angry about this.* A person's lack of meaning may feel so intense that it makes her lash out with physical force at even innocent people. She will know little about this cause of her violence. So will others, including mental health workers, until they know how the lack of meaning operates in each case and how to rectify this. They have heard for many years that *their client's chief complaint is that their lives lack meaning.* Their first task in therapy is to clarify what is meaning in general and the sources of it. (See Parts I-IV.) Then they need to attempt to restore those sources that the client lacks, realizing fully that she will be highly emotional about this. Psychologist Viktor Frankl proposed in his *Man's Search for Meaning* that meaning could be a theory of psychotherapy, but he was rather sketchy about this in view of how hopeless and helpless many of us feel. (See Sections 67 and 68 on Frankl.) Some of his followers have likewise developed a sketchy therapy of the meaning of life, emphasizing recovering from suffering and dealing with death. I cannot develop such a therapy here because of lack of space and expertise.

Another part of the life-or-death question that is deeply affected by meaning is physical health. Recently researchers have determined that *people who have meaning (usually in the sense of "purpose") tend to be healthier and live longer.* Having such meaning provides preventive health for such illnesses as high blood pressure and heart diseases. Of course, the cause of a disease is physical and genetic, but a patient's mental attitude or the meaning that she thinks her life has can make a huge difference in preventing and recovering from any diseases.

Thus, *every person fundamentally demands sufficient meaning for her to continue living her life in a nonviolent and healthy way.*

8

THE COMMON-SENSE APPROACH

These topics sound quite deep and heavy, but *my approach will be that of common sense* (= sound practical judgments that do not deny obvious reality) rather than scholarly analysis, which quickly kills a subject's spirit. I will not try to write truths that have no exceptions, but *life-truths that apply to a typical person* (= *a middle-class American who has some college education).* She is the "target audience" of this book, as marketers put it.

The common-sense approach simplifies reading and comprehension. I hope that it does not oversimplify the material. Common sense relies on what seems undeniable, for example, the existence of the external world. This book will be considerably harder to understand and more advanced than common sense, but this will be my approach to developing the idea of meaning. The laws of logic will test which conflicting views of common sense are most meaningful (in the sense of "truer"). (See Section 70 and Appendix 1 on logic.)

Common sense dictates that I will cover only main points, not all the details and exceptions to them. *I will be to-the-point and as brief as I can. Background information will be as short as needed* to give the reader working knowledge about possibly unfamiliar topics. Some critics will call me "superficial," but I prefer that label to tediously elaborating boring details and unneeded abstractions, as I was trained to do in graduate school.

9

MY START OF MAKING MEANING

I myself—although this expression sounds redundant, I shall use it whenever I describe my own experiences of making meaning-- began seeking meaning in my early teens, earlier than most people, with my internal rages for meaning. (See Section 1.) These rages were largely caused by neglect on the part of my parents. Their neglect was not malicious: they simply did not know how to show love as parents. Like almost all others in their generation, Dad and "Ma" had no training in parenting and they had no role models other than their own immigrant parents. All that they provided me was my material needs and an indoctrination in Roman Catholicism on the grade and high school levels. My parents never talked to me about going to college. They did not know what a graduate school is. So I financed the last two schools myself by a combination of scholarships and part-time work.

Even as a child, I knew that there was much more to life than what I got in my childhood. I much wanted to see the world, but I never was taken more than eighty miles from home. We went nowhere except to relatives' homes and church. I never saw downtown Chicago. My nuclear family (mother, father, and children) went to one restaurant, but only after an uncle had badgered my father into it. Dad hated both these experiences.

My father was a binge alcoholic. He often embarrassed me in front of my friends and relatives. Once my mother made me go with him to prevent him from going to a tavern. This ploy failed. In the bar I asked Dad for a Coke, but the barkeeper did not hear his slurred voice asking for it. Dad then used the quarter that he put on the bar for my Coke to subsidize his next beer. I was thirsty that hot summer day, *but I was thirsting more for meaning in my young life.*

My mother was weak-willed and depressed. I never got a hug, kiss, or word of praise despite my compliant behavior at home and high grades in school. All I got was criticisms and complaints.

If even my own parents treated me as all but worthless, how could my life matter much to anyone or even me? Questions like this started my rages and then my asking the meaning-question and finally to my making meaning for others and myself in ways that I will describe in this book.

At least *the great city of Chicago would be the setting* in which I would make meaning. Not only does it have tremendous artistic and cultural resources which I love profoundly (see Sections 21-24), but also it is the most typical of all cities in the United States in its beliefs, mostly because of its central location in the heartland. Chicago is the central city of the typical American. As I shall show, *the study of meaning ought to belong mostly to the typical person* whom, although deeply flawed, can make much meaning.

My making meaning did not arise only from negative factors such as neglectful parents. *Most of it arose from my profound love of life and living things* that I wanted to wrest as much meaning as I could from these, for examples, I cultivate flower gardens and the arts because they create beautiful, abundant, and fascinating life.

PART II

SOME MAIN SOURCES
OF MEANING

10

EIGHT SOURCES OF MEANING

The next fourteen sections of this book will treat eight main sources of meaning from which anyone can make meaning in her life. *A "source" is (=) "a large area of our lives from which we can have and make meaning"* because it can have highly significant impacts on us. I will first briefly summarize each source. Then I will describe how to make meaning and the difficulty in doing so. Finally, I will briefly describe my own efforts to make meaning in each source.

In this Part, I will discuss the following sources of meaning which are not ranked in order of importance for everyone—there is no such order: (1) quality relationships, (2) a sense of community, (3) dialogue or genuine two-way conversation, (4) fulfilling work, (5) interpreting emotions and ideas in artworks. I will treat source (6) God as a potentially huge source of meaning by offering us an immortal afterlife of joy with one's loved ones by critically examining the arguments for and against the God-question (= whether or not God externally exists?) in Part III of this book. Part IV will cover the sources of (7) material possessions and their shortcomings and (8) intangibles (= nonphysical ideas and values and arguments for them and how to know and test them).

There are many other sources of meaning (see Section 40 for a list of some of these), but these eight are some of the main ones.

11

SOURCE OF MEANING #1: QUALITY RELATIONSHIPS

Relationships to other people are our first and biggest source of meaning. "A one-on-one interactions of a self with an other" define (=) "a relationship." These start as simple events, but even as such they involve complex intangibles, for examples, the self, goodness, love, and justice.

We all need some sort of relationship with another person. *Humans are highly social animals* by their evolution and needs. Many of us have such a strong need to be with others that we endure abuse longer than seems reasonable to outsiders. Relationships to such people as our parents, siblings, fellow workers, relatives, and friends compose what religious philosopher Martin Buber called "our world." Without others, we would feel very lonely and have no support and consolation when we need these. In short, our lives without relationships would lack much meaning.

Despite the meaning (in the sense of "significance") of our relationships to us, we know little about them that we can generalize about. Common interests are likely to attract people together, yet these are certainly not required. Opposite personalities complement and also attract each other. We do know on the common-sense level that *it is often quite hard for two people to get along well.* A pair of people often must accept huge differences between each other to have a lasting relationship. We tend to instinctively fear others as competitors for limited resources, especially money. How can a person make a relationship meaningful?

In quality or good relationships, we regard others as having special meaning (in the senses of "significance" and "value"), not as just things to be used. What attracts two people together seems to be mostly meaningful emotions. Two people need to feel attracted to each other in some way. Since what draws us together are emotions, we cannot explain this attraction well in words. In general, attracting emotions feel positive (affirmative) about the meaning (in the sense of "uniqueness") of the other. For example, the emotion of trust, even the look of it from an other, can bring two people together and help sustain them throughout their relationship. Trust comes when the self finds the other reliable, honest, and good in general.

Perhaps I can best describe a relationship of high quality as one that "clicks" between two people.

Martin Buber

12

BUBER'S "THOU" AS THE MOST MEANINGFUL RELATIONSHIP

Buber gave what I think is the best account of the most meaningful type of relationship in what he called "*thou.*" *This archaic pronoun refers to the other as highly special, almost sacred.* Its only frequent usage today is to refer to God.

First, Buber required for what he metaphorically (= an implied comparison between two similar things) called "meeting" a thou is that you "hold your ground." I interpret "meeting" as "engaging the other in a personal way" and "hold your ground" as "not being afraid of talking about a meaningful (in the

27

senses of "serious" or "deep") topic." Some people have almost literally run away from me when I say, "Hi!" Buber wrote that then you "turn your whole being toward" (pay full attention to?) the other to overcome being self-centered. He called this profoundly "saying thou."

Buber surprisingly stated that "all real living is meeting." He seems to be saying here that we are only really (fully?) alive when we meet a thou. He emphasized that such a meeting happens only by grace. He also emphasized that this occurs "when you least expect it." In other words, a relationship to a "thou" is highly spontaneous.

Buber preferred his metaphorical way of speaking to scientific explanations which he thought degrade relationships (and much else) to only the physical. He regarded poetic words as more suitable to express meaningful ideas about human relationships. We all should likewise strive to speak as poetically, especially in meter and simple but special words, to make meaningful relations with others.

A person bares her soul when she meets a "thou." These meetings are so intimate that they can reveal a part of a person's meaning. They are always brief, solemn occurrences, to him.

Buber's favorite example of a "thou," which he mentions in many of his many books, is when a young girl, probably his babysitter, told him in a firm tone of voice that his mother had run away with a soldier and that she would not return to her son. Young Buber then realized that he had to establish the grounds for trusting others on his own. He did so with his notion of "thou."

The meaning of the other in Buber's "thou" is whatever is unique in the situation, as in his preceding example. You do not have to be Moses: just be yourself. I think that Buber well describes our relationships at their most meaningful (in the sense of "best") by pinpointing human connections in a concrete way.

Another way in which relationships can be highly meaningful is called "*flesh-and-blood thinking." This way calls on a self to visualize or look at the expressive aspect of the other. When the self does this, she "sees" that the other is very much like her with similar needs and problems.* Abstract thinking, on the other hand, tends to demonize the other into such categories as competitor, threat, and even witch.

Mark Twain

An example of flesh-and-blood thinking comes from writer Mark Twain's novel *Huckleberry Finn*. At first Huck is very prejudiced against the runaway slave Jim and calls him "nigger." However, while living on a raft in the Mississippi River with him, Huck comes to "see" by concrete "flesh-and-blood thinking" that Jim has his same fundamental goal of freeing himself from his oppressors in society. They become close friends working on their common goal of getting this freedom. That they do not succeed in this at the end is due to the failure of their society to engage enough in such thinking. The prejudice toward American blacks is still a terrible problem in the U. S., of course.

Even if we ourselves do not use Twain's flesh-and-blood thinking or "say thou" and "meet a thou" as Buber did, we can *think about these ideas as goals to strive toward in making meaningful relationships.*

13

RELATIONSHIPS LACKING MEANING: BUBER'S "IT"

Buber contrasted the relationship of the "thou" with what he called an "it." *Treating the other as an "it" uses her as a mere means to the self's end which benefits only the self. This definitely dehumanizes and depersonalizes the other. We all deeply resent being treated as an "it."* Buber stated that the "it" is bad only when it dominates our relationships since it is unavoidable in some situations, for example, a retail transaction. There is little doubt that the "it" dominates the relationships in the current time. Treating the other as an "it" causes many of our relationships to lack meaning. No wonder that many people today are driven to their smartphones for virtual friends on Facebook, Twitter, texting others who are a few feet away, and the like! However, a virtual friendship is only slightly more meaningful than being related to as an "it." (See Section 17 for more on this.)

Examples of the "it" relationship are legion: a macho man who has a very narrow sense of what it is to be a male; any man and any woman who regards a sexual partner only as a mere object to gratify his physical pleasure; and business down-sizers who care little when they terminate many employees. Did you ever have someone ask, "How are you?" and then cut you off as soon as you start to tell them? I have been, more than once. My final example: in the two *Weekend at Bernie's* movies (1989 and 1993), his friends do not even recognize that he is dead!

All of us have been used as an "it" in degrading relationships. *We cannot make these "its" meaningful, but we can try to avoid them as often as we can.*

Any person can make more meaning simply by emphasizing the good impact that a quality relationship can have for her and the other. For example, being kind (or what is today called "nice") in a close relationship can make more meaning daily. *Successfully doing so depends heavily on the other's cooperating. The self obviously cannot control this, although she can influence it somewhat.*

14

MY RELATIONSHIPS LACK MEANING

I myself have never met a "thou," except my dear and giving wife Mary and my children. The closest that I have come elsewhere to Buber's "saying thou" was to somberly reflect on my lowly income with a receptionist who told me about his. This exchange did not reveal any truths about the meaning of my life. Nor did it affect what Buber called the "groundswell of my being," but it did encourage me that anyone may be willing to discuss the meaning.

I myself have been treated as an "it" in many relationships outside my family. Perhaps I am too sensitive about this, but many other people feel similarly about being treated as an "it." *Few people, outside their nuclear families, now consistently regard the other as an end or value in herself.*

My clearest example of being treated as an "it" comes from my twenty-four years (and counting) of heading a teaching organization of philosophy professors which mostly holds biannual conferences and talks with comrades about philosophy. It turned out that almost all professors who joined wanted to present papers so that they would get pay raises, promotions, and tenure from their colleges for doing so. In other words, they sought only self-aggrandizement. *Almost everyone acts to take care of themselves and their nuclear families first. They do not often get to caring for others.*

Being neglected and feeling unloved as a child, I much lacked self-confidence and had what is now called "severe social anxiety." My first relationships were very hard and painful. I overcame this only after I taught for years, but some of my social anxieties still remain.

My relationships with others outside my nuclear family went poorly. I have never made a good (two-way) friend, although I have some friends and I know many people. I tried hard for many years to make new friends, mostly by sending many letters and e-mails to professors of philosophy.

I do have a small group of loyal friends who have attended my monthly Seekers' Dialogues for over twenty-four years. For these I write extended dialogues (summarized in Section 18) between a Seeker of Meaning and a typical person whom I call "Typper." These written dialogues take me a long time to write, but they give the Seekers something concrete to learn and remember for every dialogue. (Most of these "Written Dialogues" are available by contacting <u>seekerofmeaning@yahoo.com</u>.) Despite this work, attendance was rarely above ten. Only one Seeker has contacted me for friendly purposes.

I have felt profoundly lonely most of my life, especially regarding discussing ideas. This may well be the price that I must pay for obsessively seeking to make meaning. Yet, I take great joy in knowing that I am the only one, perhaps ever, who has explicitly tried to develop the idea of meaning. I feel sad about my loneliness, but *I feel heartbroken for people who cannot or do not want to make meaning in relationships.*

As I have mentioned, there are many types of relationships, for examples, parent, child, sibling, relative, friend, acquaintance, co-worker, neighbor, and many others. I obviously cannot treat these here because of limits of space.

Hands in Unity

15

SOURCE OF MEANING #2:
A SENSE OF COMMUNITY

The next source of meaning is community. The sense in which I will be using this word is (=) "a group of people who feel a sense of fellowship and common purpose." People in a community feel close to each other: they know one another on a first-name basis. Thus, a community complements a tight-knit family. Members often feel as if others in a community are almost literally an extension of themselves.

Respect for the other is high in a community. So is caring and compassionate listening. All these traits help a community reach its common goals. It fulfills our need to belong to a group since we are, again, thoroughly social animals. A community connects a person to others who are pursuing something meaningful together. *Everyone ought to try to be a member of at least one community.*

Establishing a wider sense of community can help, perhaps much, to overcome the horrific narcissism (near-total self-centerness) of our times when almost everyone seems concerned largely with themselves (and their nuclear families), which has been increasing year after year. It tells people to isolate themselves in their own wants and luxuries, certainly not the good of others, but this surely contradicts the social nature of humans.

Many people will protest that they "don't have the time" for being a part of a community because they have too much stress (undue pressure), mostly due to the time that they need to devote to working to pay their bills. This is surely true for many workers today, but creating a sense of community does not usually require much time, only the attitude that this meaning matters much.

With today's spectacular technology for communicating, we much need to extend a sense of community to the entire world, especially in regard to the globalization of the economy. This phenomenon has had devastating effects on the meaning of workers' lives because it has led to the search around the world, especially China and Mexico, for those who will work for the lowest wages. Now the owners of the main businesses throughout the world are willing to exploit workers and the world's natural resources for their own financial profit, as philosopher Karl Marx predicted in the nineteenth century. "To heck with a global community in which a worker receives a living wage," these owners now proclaim.

Social scientists are now telling us that people are happier and healthier when they give to others. These people thereby make more meaning for others and themselves. Rugged individualists, who were proposed for the U.S. by writers Ralph Waldo Emerson and Walt Whitman, now predominate our society. They get meaning exclusively for themselves. These individualists border on selfishness and even greed while they strictly conform to society's standards. They thereby end up with less meaning since they get it only for themselves.

The sense of community in our society is declining precipitously during the last few decades of economic downfall. Social scientist Robert D. Putman in his *Bowling Alone* calculates this decline at approximately fifty per cent. *Communities are rapidly being replaced by what I call "collections"* (= groups of people who are motivated mostly by self-centered purposes). A person gets much less meaning (in the senses of "love" and "caring") in a collection of people than in a community.

16

FOUR WAYS TO RESTORE COMMUNITY

I will now offer four ways in which we can restore more of a sense or feeling of community by making meaning.

First, what we most need to turn a collection into a community is a change in attitude. Of course, this is easier to say than to do. However, *creating a community becomes easier if we regard others as having much meaning*. If we do this, our attitudes will not be so self-centered. The benefits of such a change are enormous compared to those of a collection. Much meaning (especially in the sense of "fulfilling a purpose") can feel fantastic if a community achieves its goal. People in a collection feel little of this for anyone outside their nuclear families.

The second way is to *devote one-half hour a day to community service as an ideal at least*. During that time, you need to "blow up your [cable] TV" [and smartphone], as singer-songwriter John Prine advised, for a short period each day to give back to society. We can volunteer in many ways that make more meaning for others. Tutoring is at the top because it helps young minds develop. *We can do little things every day to make meaning in our neighborhoods*, for example, picking up litter (which I do almost every day) and contacting neighbors for conversation.

I make a metaphorical "community" with the environment by feeding wild birds every day—getting entertained by their behavior in the process. By doing this, I feel that I am helping other creatures have slightly more meaning at the start of each day. I feed birds until they stop coming to remind me to keep serving all day even if it is to others than humans.

I try to be as visible as possible whenever I do community service so that others will imitate me. Also, I always conspicuously carry a book in public so that others can see such intelligent actions are being done. I firmly believe that *many people who see me will do similar deeds. Humans are highly imitative animals who are strongly influenced by what they see others do.* Much making meaning in public often has the umbrella effect (= spreading like rain hitting an umbrella). Why not then do such actions for others to see and then imitate them?

Plato

My third way to restore community draws from the Plato's philosophy of a just (fair) society in his long dialogue, *The Republic.*

In a nutshell, he advocated a synthesis of his three main classes of people (guardians, enforcers and workers) to transform a collection into a just community (See Diagram #1). First, the guardians or rulers with the highest one being a philosopher-king (today called "leaders") ought to use their talented faculty of reason (thinking) to know ideas about what is just. Secondly, the enforcers (today's "police" and "military") who have strong wills need to implement these rational ideas about justice. Thirdly, governed by their emotions, the workers should feel good about being just to others in the community by doing their work. *Having meaning makes us feel happy and good in general.* If we today can achieve a synthesis of these three main classes, *we will make what Plato called a "balanced" and "healthy" community as opposed to an unbalanced and unhealthy collection of people.* Who would not prefer a healthy community to a sick collection? We should therefore seek to synthesize or harmonize people organically connected to create a just community, as Plato proposed.

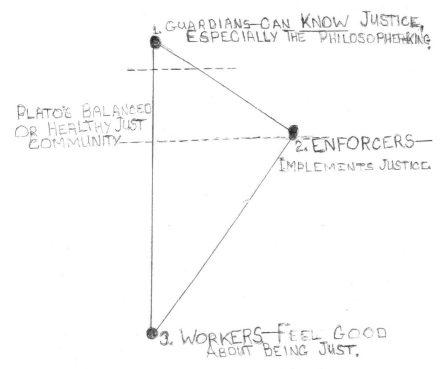

1. GUARDIANS—CAN KNOW JUSTICE, ESPECIALLY THE PHILOSOPHER-KING

PLATO'S BALANCED OR HEALTHY JUST COMMUNITY

2. ENFORCERS— IMPLEMENTS JUSTICE.

3. WORKERS—FEEL GOOD ABOUT BEING JUST.

Diagram #1: Plato's philosophy of the synthesis of a just community (for a very similar diagram the main faculties of a just individual, see Section 62.)

A fourth way to restore community is to motivate people to do so. To do this, we first need to teach them about meaning in a community versus that in a collection. Then *we need to give reasons that make people enthusiastic about joining communities.* Motivation can make a person desire more of a sense of community (and anything positive), but it is rarely offered. As Plato would put it, motivation "moves one's soul." *Appealing to emotions and desires motivates more powerfully than reasoning if these can be known and used. The most powerful emotional motivators are love (pleasure) and hate (pain).*

17

MY SEEKING MEANING
IN COMMUNITY

My making meaning in communities began in a quite rocky and discouraging way. In high school I joined many clubs, especially the newspaper and yearbook. Without my participation, these last two may well not have existed those years. None of my 168 classmates would have these concrete meaningful memories. My exhibits for the stamp club in the library graphically taught about the world's nations the many students who had study hall there. I was beginning to get much meaning from communities that I did not get from my relationships.

Unfortunately, I attended all my high school varsity football and basketball games in an unsatisfying and misdirected search for a community that I could belong to. I was following my father's near-addiction to spectator sports because he was my only role model. When he rejected my educated advance into this community, I sought my own that had more meaning for me by far.

In college I searched for a community by writing weekly columns and features about such topics as ending the Viet Nam War and many reviews of books and all the arts, including symphonic concerts, which students in the School of Music did not appreciate at all, probably because I wrote about the music's meaning and I misused some technical terms.

As an officer in student government, I proposed a student strike against the authoritarian administration—after all this was the turbulent year of 1968! My efforts in this area had meager results. They were quickly reversed when society soon changed drastically from hippies to yuppies. I did not seek meaning in politics again. *I limited my seeking community to areas in which I could realistically make meaning (in the sense of "a difference"), certainly not on the college, urban, national, or international levels. These areas are simply much too big for me and other typical people to make meaning.* I emphasize that *everyone ought to start working for a community social meaning at the smallest level in which she can make more meaning for others, and then proceed to the biggest one at which she can do so.* Every person, including a typical one, ought to seek to live the most meaningful life that she can, but she ought to not feel obligated to change the world or to aim at any other goal that is too big to attain. The main point is that we all need to make as much meaning (in the sense of "good,") especially for others on the highest level that each of us can.

My search for meaning in a community hit its lowest point when I pledged a fraternity. I did this because I had little social life, not because I was fond of parties, drinking beer, and intramural sports. I wasted much time and lowered my grades hanging out with my so-called "brothers." This was meaningful to me at the time only subjectively (because I felt quite lonely amid the glamor of college), but not objectively as I did little that was worthwhile with my frat. *I regret pledging almost as much as my supporting spectator sports, but I forgive some of it as learning to make meaning the hard way which is by experience. This is often costly.* It should be avoided whenever possible in favor of knowing how to make meaning on the first try.

My first attempts to create community outside my own schools also fared poorly. I was resisted (and even cursed) by two school boards and a fathers' club. They all wanted things done the same ineffective ways that they had always been done. I felt hurt and discouraged, but I was encouraged by the little meaning (in the sense of "improvements") that I did make for the students and the schools.

My next effort at creating community was organizing my neighborhood. When the proposed president of the revived local community organization, Hamlin Park Neighbors—Hannibal Hamlin was Abraham Lincoln's vice president—backed out at the last minute, I foolishly accepted the post without any training or experience in community organizing. I wrote two-to-six-page monthly newsletters, which I named "The Hamlin Parker," delivered to every house by volunteers whom I called "Hamlin's Heroes." *This newsletter helped the neighbors be more informed, concerned, active, and proud about where they lived.* Imagine if all neighbors had this meaning in their 'hoods!

Most people living in a big city today barely know their next-door neighbors, even their last names. A community organization gives them many reasons to get together for the good of the neighborhood, for examples, local economic development, safety, elections, parks, property taxes, city services, and schools. I was pettily criticized by a group of conservative older women known as "the Biddies," but the creation of a community was enough to propel me to lead the organization for five years until new leaders were cultivated to direct it. Over twenty years later Hamlin Park Neighbors continues strong, as it has recently purchased new playground equipment.

I was able to do all this organizing, even though I was extremely busy preparing lectures and grading hundreds of papers, journals, and exams, plus pursuing my many other sources of meaning. One of my main motivations to organize is that if I did not create a local community, no one else would. I had to "make time" (= set aside some time to do a priority) to make meaning, as we all must do. (See Section 45 on time and meaning.)

I had to move because the area where Hamlin Park Neighbors drove out gun-toting gangs soon got sky-high increases in their property taxes in return. My new neighborhood is poorer by far, but it has many classic Chicago bungalows, which I consider the ideal single-family home due to such features as their craftsmanship, solidity, design, materials, but humbleness.

I found another way to create a community organization when a local pastor who had youths distribute 10,000 fliers for their basketball camp included my neighborhood newsletter. The first time, I made the mistake of only announcing an organizing meeting. Only seven people attended, but one of them became a friend who went to many plays with me and got a part-time job for my son. So at least I got meaning from a quality relationship, but I failed to create a community this time.

My second attempt at organizing my new neighborhood was more successful by far. My neighborhood newsletter this time included several motivating ideas about creating community that I had wanted to write for years. Let me cite a few of these, since they deal with how to make more meaning in a community and in general:

* *Why not leave your society and the world a little better for your having existed?*
* *Isn't a person on earth ideally to help as many people as she can?*
* *Be a voice, a face, and a name, not an anonymous number* such as an address.

I also mentioned in the newsletter some ways to help create community in the neighborhood during the summer, for examples, sitting on your front porch, planting flowers to beautify your front yard for everyone who passes by it, saying "Hi!" to everyone, and maintaining your home so that neighbors will do likewise.

After these expressions of meaning, the new community organization took off. About eighty people attended one meeting, which was broadcast on cable TV several times, on a frigid night in January. We elected a progressive Latina "alderman" instead of the long-term mayoral-machine one. Some young members joined after learning about the organization on its Facebook page which posted neighborhood notices daily to thousands of its "friends." They will probably carry on the meaning of neighbors working together for common goals for many years. This is another example of the umbrella effect. (See Section 16.)

Today many "communities" are being created on the Internet, which also gives us access to enormous amounts of information—but not much worthwhile knowledge—and mountains of grammatically weak e-mail. This sadly seems enough for many people. These are called "virtual" communities, but they are not even that. Professor Sherry Turkle in her *Reclaiming Conversation* notes that virtual communities "offer the illusion of companionship without the demands of friendship." The 'net lacks *the primary trait of a community: a caring human presence relating in person to others and working toward common goals with them. Nothing can substitute for the meaning of such a human presence.*

I have worked hard to create communities mostly because a person can thereby make much meaning for others.

18

SOURCE OF MEANING #3: DIALOGUE

Once in either a community or a relationship a major task will be to communicate feelings, ideas, and goals. I firmly believe that the best way to do this is through talking, if it is possible in a situation. *Talk has a vocal human ingredient lacking in other forms of communication. In talking we deal with real human presences with such factors as their facial expressions, emotional responses, and especially tones of voice. These often reveal what is meaningful to the speaker. One human talking to another with give-and-take to clarify, inquire, and the like is precious and often the best way to communicate meaning, often superior even to the written word.* Talk can be a fruitful source of objective meaning if it takes the form of what Buber called "dialogue" defined as (=) "a two-way exchange of meaningful (in the senses of 'big' and 'serious') ideas and feelings."

Instead of dialogue we usually talk about little more than trivia and information that we need for our survival, but not our prospering. People often verbally exchange social niceties, light topics, trivial matters, gossip—most people are nosy—, personal experiences, politics on all levels and personal news (if any). This is called "chit chat." Yak! Yak! Yak! Such talk has only a little subjective meaning.

I myself believe that many people do not engage in dialogue, especially in their responses to questions, because *they often use talk to express their own unfulfilled wants and interests, subconscious desires, and other varieties of lack of meaning. We frequently want to express verbally our urgent need for more meaning.* Little meaning or communication takes place in such a monologue (one-way conversation) except subjectively to the one who monologues.

There are several guidelines for dialogue. People frequently and flagrantly violate them because of their ignorance and their unfulfilled quest for meaning through talk. For example, many people continue to talk about tangents, which violates Guideline #4 below. Digressing goes hopelessly far from the original topic which will be very hard to discuss again.

Dialogue is an extremely hard goal to reach; even everyday conversation is a rocky road with many pitfalls. The following are some main guidelines for engaging in dialogue:

1. Talk about *a serious subject*, although humor is meaningful in itself and helpful to relieve a heavy tone;

2. Talk about *a broad (big) subject* to address much meaning and to avoid trivia (See Section 33 on the limits of materialism.);

3. Each person *ought to talk about half the time* or two-way, neither person should dominate the conversation as in a monologue;

4. *Stay on the topic* until it is finished, do not follow tangents because they quickly go very far from the topic;

5. *Do not interrupt unless necessary*, for examples, if the other person is saying something false or irrelevant; and

6. *Always reply directly* to what has just been said at least briefly to acknowledge it and the person who said it.

My own experience with talk has been poor. I myself have rarely had a dialogue. Few people have wanted to discuss serious topics with me. Like almost everyone, I would now have a hard time holding a dialogue because I have had so little practice in doing it.

Twenty-three years ago I formed a monthly discussion group that I named "the Seekers" to have dialogues mostly about meaning and personal philosophy of life. At first I recruited professors of philosophy, but very few attended despite the fact that they all want their students to talk about philosophy in class. So I promoted the Seekers at the College of Complexes, a weekly group for discussing mostly social issues in which I have been a regular attendee for over thirty years. Several from this group wanted to learn and talk about philosophy on a long-term basis. Together with a few of my friends, we held interdisciplinary dialogues almost every month since then. I had to organize and direct the Seekers so I could have authentic dialogues.

19

SOURCE OF MEANING #4: FULFILLING WORK

Work is a huge source of positive and negative meaning because we spend so much of our waking time and energy at it.

A job ideally should embody a worker's main purpose in life. Recall that "purpose" is the main sense of "the meaning of life." (See Section 3.) So much of the meaning of a person's life has to do with her work or career. How sorrowful that so few people find the purpose of their lives in their work!

I emphasize that each person much needs to determine what is most meaningful (in the sense of "likes") to her that could possibly be groomed into a job.

Meaningful work has eluded most people throughout the ages of history. This is especially true now in the fields of business and service, which currently comprise over seventy-five per cent of the workforce in the U.S. (whose labor laws largely favor employers, unlike many countries). Much personal meaning is taken out of jobs by making them computerized and mechanized, as brilliantly prefigured in the stopwatch Nazi gas chamber scene in the movie *Schindler's List* (1993). No wonder that so many workers spend so much of their free time escaping from their jobs! (See Section 42 on escapes from meaning.)

In the most honest account of work yet, *Working*, writer Studs Terkel emphasized that work often humiliates and commits "violence to a worker's spirit as well as to the body" (page xiii). I agree most jobs do not supply workers enough meaning (in the senses of "purpose" and "fulfillment" from developing one's highest potentials).

There is little chance of changing the nature of work since it is so economically profitable to owners, especially of mega-corporations (called "the 1 per cent" by critics of capitalism). However, companies such as Ben & Jerry's have implemented strategies to make work more meaningful to workers, for examples, by managing, negotiating for, and even owning their workplaces.

The broader that a job is, such as working with people, the more meaning that accrues to a worker. So many jobs today are overspecialized, again only to make profits for the owners. Few workers now see a project from beginning to end, as did the first shoemakers, according to Terkel. Today many jobs are just tasks that need to be done to survive. These can have little meaning. A job that is mostly just a paycheck leaves a deadening emptiness at the core of a worker's life. As policeman Renault Robinson told Terkel, "It gets pretty dull" (page 200).

At least workers can get some meaning (in the sense of "importance") from doing their jobs well and helping others even in small ways. These give workers a sense accomplishment and hence pride in their work.

The most meaningful job would coincide with what a person wants to do in her free time such as read or help others. In other words, *your vocation ideally should match your avocation (hobby). It should also match your skills,* whether these be intellectual, artistic, social, manual, or any other. Terkel has made the distinction that *workers do not want a job so much as a calling in life (page xxviiii). They desire in their depths to do something meaningful (in the sense of "worthwhile") with their working lives.*

Terkel's skillful interviews with workers made him conclude that *what they found most meaningful is to leave something to show that they were here (page xxx),* for examples, buildings made by a construction worker, businesses enabled by a real estate investor, and accomplished children nurtured by a housewife. Terkel emphasized that he was "constantly astonished by the extraordinary dreams of ordinary people" (page xxix).

A job is meaningful whenever it betters society, even slightly. Meaningful work is one of the greatest goals that people want much, but few attain to a high degree. Concentrating on finding a fulfilling career as early as one can obviously help much to make meaning in this very important source, although far too few young people do this or develop their interests along vocational lines. Alas! This massive sorrow results directly from our neglect of the explicit idea of meaning as applied to work.

20

MY MAKING MEANING IN WORK

Like everyone, I myself implicitly sought meaning in work throughout most of my life. My first job started in freshman year of high school delivering morning newspapers from bright yellow carts. I saw the city about to begin its day fraught with degrees of meaning. The meaning of my work was simple at the start: to work mostly at factories within walking distance of my parents' isolated home (actually a "flat" or one floor of a two-story house) to make enough money for my minimal needs then. I loved this, but I knew even then that work should have more meaning by far than this simplicity.

I found this meaning in work at age twenty-five when I became a professor teaching philosophy (and English) in Massachusetts. *I would get much meaning for more than forty years teaching the fundamental ideas about life to young people.*

Professors are retained mostly by publishing useless articles in scholarly journals that only a few professors read or understand. So I tried to publish such articles. I almost got my revised PhD dissertation on a completion of Cohen's principle of polarity (opposites that attract each other) published as a book by Princeton University Press.

My first published article was entitled "The Meaning of Life" in a journal sent to most colleges in the U.S. by land speculator Alfred Koenig. He published, without suggesting that I edit a word, twelve more of my essays mostly developing the ideas of the meaning of life and personal philosophy.

At the same time I tried without any training or mentoring to become an excellent teacher. Most of my students had poor reading and writing skills. It was not highly rewarding to teach them. The interested students were highly appreciative and rewarding.

I spent much of almost every day for the next forty years preparing for class the next day. I enjoyed this much because I was studying ideas with a view toward implicitly developing the idea of meaning. This gave all my preparing

for classes big purpose. I always oriented it toward settling my
rages. (See Section 1.)

The idea of meaning slowly emerged from my daily prepara
I teach a section on the meaning of life itself in my introductor
try to *teach meaning for all topics in the indirect way of emphasizing their significant impacts*—recall that this is my definition of "meaning"—on students' daily lives. (See Section 2.) This became the most effective part of my teaching. Most sadly, some young students do not care about meaning—or anything else!—but most did because *teaching for meaning motivates learning* by emphasizing the effects that studying this idea can have for them.

I am so intent on spreading the gospel of meaning and philosophy that I demand that my students learn much. In other words, I am what students commonly call "hard." Some students try to make trouble for such professors. Even teaching meaning cannot perform miracles of transforming students who totally do not want to be.

An extended example of my teaching meaning is what is human nature. I teach how this idea has much meaning (in the senses of "impact" and "implication") for a student's attitude toward all people, including herself. Please see Appendix II for a hand-out for the first class on human nature (and ethics) as an example of how I teach meaning indirectly. I give such hand-outs as my lectures in all my courses. (The blanks provide forums for discussions in class to fill them in.) (Also see Appendix II for the introductory hand-out on ethics.)

Part of my pedagogy (teaching methods) for teaching meaning consists of giving many specific examples for all philosophical problems and ideas to apply these abstractions to the physical world. Another pedagogical technique that gives ideas concrete meaning is drawing diagrams for most of them on the blackboard or Smartboard (its electronic version). (See Diagrams I and III on Plato's philosophy of the just society and individual.) Yet another technique is never to select a topic that is too large, theoretical, or technical for students to find meaningful (in the sense of "relevant"), for examples, political philosophy (too big) and deduction (too technical). These are some of the techniques or methods that I developed to make meaning teaching philosophy.

I got tremendous meaning (in the sense of "fulfillment") from my work in teaching over 7,000 young people topics that many of them will think about and improve on for the rest of their lives. The ones who keep in contact with me, some for over forty years, made meaning in major ways, usually fulfilling careers, often in the ministry. The students who "got" the idea of meaning found it outstanding. There is hardly a more gratifying feeling than being praised for one's work. Teaching meaning makes a dramatic difference to students' basic beliefs that improve the quality of their lives. What better reason can there be for working?

21

SOURCE OF MEANING #5:
INTERPRETING ART

Art, more specifically, (=) the fine arts (not the practical ones) of expressing unique feelings and ideas in a concrete form, is a gigantic source of meaning to me mostly because of its enormous creativity and imagination, both of which I will explain soon below. These two factors make art the most subjective source of meaning because people have very different views about artworks and very few objective standards for them.

I realize that most people do not get much, if any, meaning from art. They experience so little art in society today that they do not know how to appreciate it. The usual response that they get from asking an artist what her work means is, "That's up to you." However, it is really up to the artist to make works that have meaning for others and to explain or communicate clearly how they do this. (See Section 1 on the meaning-question.)

I will next briefly explain four ways, all of which are aesthetic (artistic) states of mind, in which a person can get meaning from artworks.

1. INTERPRETATIONS (=) *explain what you "get" intellectually from an artwork*. A person comes closest to identifying what an artwork means (in the sense of "signifies") to her when she makes an interpretation of it. In other words, in an interpretation a person explains what she thinks that an artwork is about or means.

To interpret any artwork, a person first needs to know something enlightening about it to her, for examples, fruitful facts about it, its place in art history, its style or school, the artist's intention, and similar knowledge. All knowledge has some meaning, but try to learn something about an artwork that interests you personally in order to interpret it more easily.

Immanuel Kant.

Second, the interpreter needs to use her imagination on this background knowledge to interpret an artwork. Her knowledge about it gives her a basis to imagine something that it means (again in the sense of "signifies") to her. Our imaginations expand widely, but they need some basis on which to begin. The richness of an artwork can suggest many different interpretations. (See examples in the third paragraph below.)

Our faculty of imagination (=) makes some sort of image, including verbal or audio as well as visual, from another one. *Using the imagination on an artwork well can have much meaning to a person because it starts her own interpretation of it.* There are no rules for how to imagine something because this depends on what philosopher Immanuel Kant in his *Critique of Aesthetic Judgment* called the "free play of the imagination." He rightly thought that this is our highest faculty, superior to even reasoning in which an idea always is limited by an opposite idea, for example, bad and good results from every major action. The imagination has no limits except to make an image.

There can be more interpretations than there are artworks since a person can make more than one for each work. *All interpretations of an artwork are welcome as long as they are based on it to some extent.* The more that an interpretation is based on an artwork, the more welcome or the better that it is. There is no "correct" or "right" interpretation as artworks are amazingly rich in the potential meanings that can be imagined in them. However, *interpretations of an artwork that stress its meaning (in the sense of its "deep feelings and ideas" explained in Sections 22 and 23) are better than those that do not.* However, we cannot call an interpretation "the best" because the meaning that an artwork can have is limitless and can always be better or fuller.

The following are a few very brief examples of interpretations of artworks: Renaissance music sounds bold just as that era was; many happy Impressionist paintings show France as such at that time; Andy Warhol's repetitious *Coca Cola Bottles* depict how materialistic the U.S. had become after World War II; Jackson Pollock's splattered and dripped paint reveals his own chaotic subconsciousness; and sculptures of some Hindu deities, for example, the dancing goddess Shiva, have multiple arms to suggest their many powers that include creating and destroying the illusion of the universe.

Shiva

Interpreting an artwork makes it far more meaningful because the *interpreter articulates in words what it means (in the sense of "signifies") to her*. Also, many artworks can be *interpreted as depicting a world better than our physical one*, for examples, all Utopian novels such as by Thomas More and the paintings of Vermeer which show tranquil, brightly lit domestic scenes where their beauty draws the viewer in. Though such worlds are imaginary, psychologists have long known that *fantasies of the imagination can seem almost as real and moving to a person as her experiences themselves*.

2. DISINTEREST comes from just perceiving artworks with one's senses, usually seeing. An artwork can be meaningful in its very appearance, as Kant again noticed, calling this phenomenon being "disinterested"—a quite confusing name since it now refers to the opposite. *Artworks can give us sensations that have meaning (in the sense of "power") to us just by being sensed. A person's favorite artworks have something fascinating for her just to behold*, for general examples in various arts, novelty, unusual shapes, haunting sounds, and boldness of forms. This fascination can come from an artwork's very materials, for general examples, subtle colors of a painting, vivid words in a poem, and graceful bodily movements in a dance.

In art there is a concentration on sheerly sensing a work for its own sake. We can enjoy just sensing, usually by our higher senses of seeing or hearing, artworks, for specific examples, the gorgeous browns in a painting by Rembrandt, the smooth skin of the marble sculptures by Michelangelo, and the harmoniously layered notes in a symphony by Mozart. Even such a simple design as the interlocking Ls of the early Hindus, which the Nazis adapted into the swastika, can "hold one's vision to the expanse that it adorns," and, "the effect of good decoration is to make the surface, somehow, more visible," according to Langer in her book, *Feeling and Form, page 61*. So we can get meaning from an artwork just by perceiving some feature in it that we find interesting or fascinating for no other reason than its sheer appearance to our senses (*Feeling and Form, page 50*). Such a simple experience and mental state as disinterest thus gives us another way to get meaning from artworks.

3. SUSPENSION (= *temporarily setting aside any practical purpose to use an artwork*) is a special meaning, as Kant yet again noticed. We also suspend all our mundane activities and chores. This can feel like a great relief from our daily troubles. *Time also seems suspended when a person experiences a meaningful artwork to her, as evidenced in the classic saying "Life is short, art is long."* This suspension can feel like a fine relief from one's tedious routines.

Architecture may seem to be an exception because it is a practical art that consists of buildings in which people live, work, worship, do business and so on. However, whenever we focus on a building's sheer form, novelty, beauty, or the like, for example, in the majesty and upward soaring of a grand Gothic cathedral, we are not regarding it as a practical thing to be manipulated, but as a work of art to be appreciated. Thus, we can get much meaning (in the sense of "fundamental significance") by suspending our utilitarian outlook, worldly activities, and sense of time to enjoy simply sensing an artwork for its own sake.

4. CREATIVITY *abounds in all the arts. It can give much meaning because it has new impacts on us.* Creativity goes beyond altering images, which the imagination does, into making new objects and ideas come into existence.

A common technique for creativity involves an artist taking a risk by combining unrelated things. Another involves her fitting parts together into a whole, like combining pieces or parts of a jigsaw puzzle.

We all are creative to some extent because we all have solved problems. A solution requires a new idea, at least to the thinker, to overcome whatever blocks it. Artists need creativity to solve artistic problems such as new use of materials, invention of new styles, and even the creation of new art genres (types) such as collage paintings by Pablo Picasso and mobiles by sculptor Alexander Calder.

Artworks create many new feelings and ideas; for example, some music in the Renaissance expresses the new idea that our lives ought to be fun as well as serve God which is all that it did in the Middle Ages. (See the third paragraph after this for more examples of new ideas in the arts and Section 65 on the meaning of life in the Middle Ages.)

A warning about the meaning of creativity in the arts: *the first time that an artwork is revolutionary and highly creative marks a meaningful (in the sense of "important") event in the history of art,* for example, painter Vassily Kandinsky's first abstract painting in 1913 when all previous paintings had imitated something realistically. However, such *creativity is no longer meaningful when it is substantially repeated once,* for example, the endless all-black paintings that many abstract painters somehow feel obligated to make.

Another warning about creativity in the arts: it is meaningful whenever an artist produces a new style of art, such as painting shocking colors and lack of perspective (indication of differences in size and distance of objects in a painting). However, *newness has more meaning (again in the sense of "significance") by far when it features a meaningful emotion or idea—see Sections 22 and 23), not just something new or different for its own sake,* for example, much modern art, such as sculptor Claes Oldenburg's giant chairs after he had made many other giant objects, is just different for its own sake with very little or no meaning (in the sense of "expressing worthwhile emotions or ideas").

To summarize this section briefly: artworks can give us meaning if a perceiver can attain four states of mind: interpretation or an explanation of an artwork by using one's imagination and background knowledge, disinterest or purely perceiving an artwork, suspension from practical purposes and time, and creativity or making new feelings and forms. Knowing each of these four states can help us get meaning from art and make our experience of an artwork meaningful if we avail ourselves to them.

These four artistic states of mind are by no means easy to attain, especially without knowledge about them. Art is surely one of hardest ways to make meaning despite that it is the most subjective source. I have not even mentioned the more complex process of making meaning by creating art.

22

ARTWORKS EXPRESS
MEANINGFUL TRUTHS (IDEAS)

Wr can interpret many artworks so that they give us meaningful truths (in the sense of "big" or "life"). *Artworks give us in sensuous, vivid, and powerful ways broad life-truths (= ideas that correspond to human life as a whole), for examples, about human nature, the self, goodness, and all values.* (See Section 35 for specific examples of intangible truths.) *All these areas are extremely hard or impossible to know by today's factual method of the sciences with its demand for physical proof.* The arts excel at expressing emotions (see Section 23), but they also excel at expressing life-truths and new ideas. Part of this poem can serve as an extended example:

"Harlem"
by Langston Hughes

What happens to a dream deferred?
Does it dry up
like a raisin in the sun?
Does it stink like rotten meat?
Maybe it sags
like a heavy load.
Or does it just explode?

Hughes' poem tells us, in very striking metaphors such as stinking rotten meat, sagging and exploding the life-truth that whenever we defer for too long our "dreams" or major purposes (definition of "meaning" #3), such as racial equality and integration, they become denied. Very long denials may "dry up like a raisin in the sun." This metaphor became the title of Loraine Hansberry's play *A Raisin in the Sun* protesting housing segregation which helped to change

54

the law allowing it in the U. S. Hughes' "Harlem" also inspired Martin Luther King's assertion that "a dream deferred is a dream denied," which became a slogan of the civil rights movement of the 1960s in the U.S. Thus, *Hughes' "Harlem" helped Hansberry, King, and us to recognize through vivid images the life-truth that we all need to act on our dreams as soon as we can* before it is too late to realize them.

Untitled, commonly called "the Chicago Picasso," in Daley Plaza

My second example of a life-truth expressed by an artwork comes from Pablo Picasso's untitled metal sculpture in the Daley Plaza of Chicago. Is this the front of a bird with its wings spread? Is it a woman with long hair? Or is it a skinny dog such as an Afghan hound? Many other interpretations are possible. *Whatever this sculpture represents, it gives us the life-truth that large cities such as Chicago are complex mysteries of diverse richness*, for examples, their ethnic populations and practices such as customs, clothing, and food. This may be a reason that Picasso's abstract sculpture has become one of the main symbols— today called "icons"—for Chicago.

Ludwig von Beethoven

I will conclude this section on *meaningful ideas expressed by the arts by showing how they can be expressed even by classical music despite its not having any words.* My example will be Beethoven's *Ninth Symphony*—which does have words in its last movement, but they do not enter into this interpretation. The start of this symphony can be interpreted by its sounds to encapsulate his mighty struggles in life, especially the losses of his "dearly beloved" and his hearing which is the worst nonfatal disease that can afflict a composer of music. He begins with orchestral sounds of turmoil and dark stormy passages that I interpret to express the loss of much meaning in his life. In the somber second movement, Beethoven musicalizes his bitterly disappointing experiences, but in a beautiful way suggesting the ability of our will to rise above them.

The third movement of his *Ninth Symphony* begins even more beautifully so that it seems to be the answer, but then is interrupted twice by fanfares from brass instruments that sound like hammer blows knocking at heaven's door—shades of the title of a Bob Dylan song and the four-note theme (da-da-da-dah) of "fate [death] knocking at the door" in Beethoven's *Fifth Symphony*!—demanding real answers. When God does not respond, this movement ends with calm acceptance.

The final movement of the *Ninth Symphony* opens with an outburst of dissonance (notes that do not harmonize) as if Beethoven intended to defy God. Instead, *he then calls upon a simple ethereal (heavenly) tune of joy* in the major (happy-sounding) key. (Going from the minor or sad-sounding key to the major one at the end is a common pattern in classical symphonies.) Out of his own will power he expresses much happiness and joy. This symphony expresses his gift to us. It results from choosing to hear the joy of his genius. Perhaps this is the reason that he set to music writer Friedrich Schiller's poem "Ode to Joy" to end this grand symphony perhaps testifying to the brotherhood or close relationship of all humans and to their free will. (See Sections 46 and 47 on the free-will question.)

Thus, the main idea that Beethoven expresses in his Ninth Symphony is that the human will is strong enough to surmount in joy even God's non-response. This affirmation of life is its main life-truth, although it has others. Beethoven's *Ninth Symphony* is also well known for its profound emotional meaning (in the senses of "intense joy, excitement and suspense"). (I owe most of this superb interpretation to my fine friend for over 35 years and an expert on classical music, D. H. Robinson.)

23

THE MEANING OF ART IS
MOSTLY EMOTIONAL

The main meaning in art is emotional, from the deepest sorrow to the greatest joy with many variations in between. The emotions are where we live most of our daily lives. *Even though we feel emotions strongly, we find it extremely hard to name them.* An artwork rarely gives explicit clues about which emotions it expresses. To be sure, fast music in general sounds happy, such as composer Edgar Elgar's "Pomp and Circumstance" frequently played at celebrations, especially graduations, or the beat-the-world march the last movement of Tchaikovsky's *Fifth Symphony.* Slow music in general sounds sad such as in "Taps" for dead soldiers and Mozart's "Requiem Mass" for his domineering father.

Words are poor at expressing an emotion because they are abstract, general, and felt weakly. For example, the words "I love you" can refer to a wide variety of emotions. Feelings, on the other hand, are concrete, particular and felt strongly; for example, Pierre Renoir's painting, *A Dance in the Country,* shows a couple engrossed in their love of each other and the music playing then. *Artworks express emotions in a very specific way,* according to composer Aaron Copland in his book, *What to Listen for in Music.* For example, a sad sonata can sound pessimistic, resigned, and other specific kinds of sadness. So, unlike words, artworks can convey emotional meaning well.

Again, the huge difficulty with this view of the meaning of art as mostly emotional is thus that humans have an extremely hard time naming or identifying even the main emotions expressed in an artwork other than joy, sorrow, fear and a few other feelings.

Pierre Renoir, A Dance in the Country

For very brief examples of expression of emotional meaning in painting, "*Nighthawks*" by Edward Hopper terrifically expresses the emotion of desolate loneliness in a city where a greasy-spoon diner cuts through the dark night with its glaring fluorescent lights and people sit at its counter as isolated from each other as they can get, and Edvard Munch's painting *The Scream* expresses the anxiety coming from the whole world that he himself felt one day and that eerily symbolizes the anxiety that many people feel in the modern era. *As Langer concisely summarized, "The [visual] arts look like our feelings feel." All the arts can express how our feelings and emotions feel extremely well in different ways.*

24

MY SEEKING MEANING IN ART: FINDING BEAUTY

 I myself have sought meaning in art intensely throughout my adult life. In the artistic richness of Chicago I have experienced innumerable artworks, mostly paintings, theater, films, and classical and acoustic music by singer-songwriters. I go to art museums frequently, usually to hear fine talks at the awesome Art Institute of Chicago. In all these activities I was making meaning (in the sense of "the imaginative expansion of the mind and emotions") for me. I find much meaning in art, as in all the examples just discussed and many more. The arts have been the largest source of meaning for me.

Beauty is the greatest meaning (in the sense of "value") that I have experienced in the arts. I wholly agree with Plato in his dialogue *The Symposium* that *beauty is "the everlasting possession of the good."* He thereby regarded beauty as higher than even the moral good because a beautiful artwork captures images of this good, for example, a hero in a sculpture, painting, or poem. We can behold such heroic beauty forever when it is physically embodied in an artwork.

Platonic beauty resides in the mathematical, especially geometrical, proportions that for some mysterious reason—even to Plato himself!—are just right, for examples, harmonious sounds from an orchestra, the majestic geometric ratios of Greek temples, and the best words and meters in poems. (See Section 35 for more about Plato on beauty as proper proportions.) As he metaphorically put it, beauty gives us "wings to soar" to highly meaningful (mostly in the sense of "profound") emotions and ideas. *There is literally no limit to the beauty (and other aesthetic values such as vividness and child-like (not childish) simplicity that we can make in our experiences of art* due to its tremendous creativity and imagination.

ART CRITICISM. Perhaps the culmination of meaning in art for me and the typical person is not beauty since that has been replaced by many other artistic values, is a bit much, and already has been done many times, for examples, in Raphael's paintings of the madonna and Michelangelo's sculpture of her in his "Pieta" (Mary holding her crucified son), but in art criticism (judging the value or worth of a work of art). *What an artwork ought to mean (in the sense of its "significant impact") to the typical person provides the judging standard of whether or not an artwork is good.* This meaning is somewhat objective in that it needs to reside in factors worthy of approval in an artwork itself. (See examples in the next paragraph and Section 48 on objective meaning.) What other standard can be more appropriate to judging an artwork?

The standard of meaning for judging the value or goodness of art works consists of all the factors treated on meaning in the arts, especially the four aesthetic states of mind (interpretation, disinterest, suspension and creativity) and the expression of emotions. These are key to the meaning of artworks.

An example of an artwork that would be judged as "beautiful" or "good" "in general" can come from Michelangelo's statue of "David" because it means much (in the sense of "significant impact") in its ideal form of the male human body showing confidence in God. Another example of a positive evaluation according to the standard of meaning can come from composer Maurice Ravel's music piece "Bolero," which he took from a lively Spanish dance that features sharp turns and foot-stomping with one-hand over the dancer's head. Ravel's score becomes louder, but not faster, as many listeners believe that it does. Its theme becomes mesmerizing in its intensity and it steams up to to its textured build up. However, the conclusion of this dance sounds like a discordant fizzle. I interpret that this ending strongly reminds listeners of times in their lives that they thought would be highly meaningful, but turned out not to be so.

According to the standard of meaning, bad art has little meaning for a variety of reasons, for example, triviality. A movie or play that appeals to the audience's prurient interest and morbid curiosity is not a good artwork according to this standard.

Many artists search intensely for meaning in their lives. Probably the most obvious example is Vincent Van Gogh. He found the night sky alive with the presence of God in his painting "The Starry Night."

I myself have practiced art criticism since freshman year of college in various newspapers and radio stations because of my great love of the arts. I have reviewed literally hundreds of art works in all genres. I have had difficulty in determining or finding a standard to judge artworks until I narrowed the standard of judgment down from "the meaning of life" to just "meaning". Now I review mostly plays only on my website meaninginart.org.

PART III

GOD AND MEANING

25

SOURCE #6: SEEKING GOD

If God (= the supernatural, supreme, and eternal being) truly or objectively exists, He would easily be the greatest source of meaning. (As God has no gender, I will use the traditional male pronoun.) Not only could He have complete control over our lives, but also *He could grant us an immortal afterlife of joy with our loved ones,* if the Abrahamic religions (Christianity, Islam, and to a much lesser extent, Judaism) are true about the afterlife. Because of this highly generous view of afterlife, God has been the biggest subjective source of meaning in the history of the western hemisphere, and most of the Middle East. (Criticism: Would not even such an afterlife become boring after a few million years or so?)

The God-question is (=) *"whether or not He exists objectively (externally) to our minds?"* (See Section 48 on the difference between subjective and objective meaning.) *There is no more meaningful question that a human can ask than whether she is really immortal or eventually just ashes* (if cremated) or food for worms (if buried in a wooden coffin). *This question has so much potential meaning that no one ought to ignore it.* Even firm atheists need to keep this question alive to themselves simply because of the potentially tremendous meaning of the endless number of years involved in the afterlife.

No belief can be more meaningful (in the senses of "optimistic" and "flattering") than such an immortal afterlife in which everything is made right for everyone in heaven. This belief can greatly console us to the horror of our deaths. On the other hand, *no belief is more terrifying than burning forever in hell for not believing in or following the commands of God.*

The main question about the meaning of God is the God-question because anything must exist externally to us to have objective or true meaning. I will therefore focus only on the God-question for this source of meaning. It is appalling how few people even raise this question. God obviously could not grant us an afterlife if He does not even exist. As writer and editor Philip Berman asserts,

"Our souls are at stake" (*The Search for Meaning, page 15*) in answering the God-question.

Since an externally existing God would be our greatest source of meaning (in the senses of "eternal joy" and "purpose"), *the question of whether or not He exists is the most complicated and the hardest to know.* Because of this and the question's supreme importance, I think that we all are obligated to seek answers to the God-question for at least a little time every day for the rest of our lives. (Jews, Christians, and Muslims can take a "day of rest," as their God did in *Genesis.* He apparently was tired after He completed His gigantic task of creating the universe!) I myself have devoted a half-hour every day for about the last forty-five years to finding the most objective answer to the God-question by talking about it, listening to talks on it in the media, but usually reading books about it.

From the point of view of meaning, God's external existence needs to be extremely hard to know. If it were not, the meaning of our lives (in the sense of their "purpose") would obviously be to utterly devote ourselves to God so that we can joyfully live with Him and our loved ones forever.

God obviously exists in the subjective sense (within our minds or thinking). This sense by itself gives very many people much meaning (in the senses of "hope" and "consolation") about God and hence their own afterlives. Yet, *belief in God's existence only in the subjective sense by itself should not give us such meaning because this God may exist only in our minds.* The s*ubjective sense of God's existence by itself can easily delude people into believing what they want to make themselves feel that they will survive in immortal bliss without any rational evidence that God and the afterlife even exist objectively.*

Belief in God in the strictly subjective sense is a blind faith (= unquestioning belief in God) that does not even attempt to answer the God-question. *If a person does not have objective reasons for thinking that God exists, then belief in Him is due to either ignorance of the quite complex issues in answering the God-question or the cowardly self-delusion of people unwilling to accept the finality of their deaths and those of their loved ones. Whereas people who have this self-delusion will live more moral and overall better lives, they do so for strictly selfish and wrong reasons. Their lives are thus false and phony at their core. I have much pity for them.*

Thinking about God explicitly in terms of His meaning is quite rare except in the subjective sense in which a person believes that her life would be meaningless or have no meaning (in the sense of "purpose") if God did not exist. Again, this belief has no objective reference whatsoever, just a person's desire to always exist and never die. It should not be mistaken for an argument for God's external (to humans) existence; it is only a plea or hope for immortal life of joy from a being not known to even exist.

BLIND AND RATIONAL FAITH. Everyone's answer to the God-question rests ultimately (in the end) on her faith. *"Faith" is a most ambiguous and troublesome* *word. Its primary usage is (=) "a strong belief and trust in something without enough evidence."* (Apostle Paul conceived of it poetically in *Hebrews Chapter 11, Verse 1* as "the essence of things not seen.") *Since a faith does not have sufficient evidence to warrant a belief, it is fundamentally non-rational, although not always irrational. As such, faith has subjective meaning. It is a strong personal bias or predisposition. In regard to the God-question, this bias can be either in favor of God's existence or in favor of metaphysical materialism (=only matter exists, God does not).*

As so subjective, a faith can feel very powerful to a person. It is almost impossible to rationally convince anyone of an opposing faith (or hence belief). However, this is a huge psychological problem regarding the tenacity to our beliefs in favor of the security of our emotions rather than a philosophical one of making the most logical or soundest argument. As physicist David Bohm wrote, when people defend their assumptions, it is "as if they are defending themselves" *(On Dialogue, page 34).*

All of our beliefs ultimately stem from our faiths about them. These faiths should not be blind, but rational in that a person rationally examines them. Such a faith in God is still possible if it is "rationally plausible" (probably true) according to Professor David Stewart in *Exploring the Philosophy of Religion, page 161). A rational faith in God can come only from carefully considering His objective existence as known by logical reasoning. If a person does this, she can have a rational (reasonable) or justified faith.* This is the best approach that we can take to the God-question in view of our quite limited power of knowing intangibles like God.

Thus, a faith is a poor place to begin to answer the God-question because it is essentially nonrational.

A faith orients people toward a key aspect of reality, but for no known reason. It is a basic assumption that each person must make for big areas of their lives to start their thinking about each. For examples (with the two main opposing choices of a faith indicated in parentheses): reality (materialism or God), knowledge (sensory experience or sheer thinking), people in general (good or bad with much that follows), politics (conservative or liberal), the future(optimistic or pessimistic) and even mathematics (Euclidean or non-Euclidean geometries).

Which one in each of these pairs of faith that a person maintains may seem arbitrary; they stem from her innermost self but this is nonrational. Faith is thus extremely meaningful (in the sense of "important") in understanding a person's basic belief from which all the others in that area follow. Very little can be done to change a faith in this sense except a major event, for example, a personal trauma, but hardly a strong argument or reason.

(What basic faith can be more rational than that our lives have meaning? None, but even this faith ought to be objectively argued, not subjectively.)

To have a rational faith in God, we need to have a strong argument, not in the sense of a "disagreement," but (=) "thinking using premises (evidence) to support a conclusion" that God exists objectively.(See Appendix I on arguments.) Only such an argument logically entitles one to believe that God exists in more than the subjective sense (one's inner desire not to die). The word "prove" has now come to signify only (=) "to give strong *physical* evidence that a belief is true." So this word can no longer apply to God's existence because He is obviously not physical. *Most people who do not believe in God (atheists, agnostics, and materialists*—see Sections 29-31) *wrongfully demand physical proof and evidence of God's existence (and everything else).* They have quite narrow and undeveloped views of whether or not we can know intangible (big) truths such as God's existence. (See Section 31 on agnostics.)

Although it is no longer correct today to say that God's existence can be "proven" (because that word now denotes only physical or concrete evidence), belief in it may still be rationally meaningful. I will next give four logical arguments for why I think that it is. While these arguments cannot rely on tangible evidence, they are grounded on intangible reasons such as objective meaning, creation of the universe, the grand design (plan) of the universe and mysticism (personal encounters with God).

26

AN ARGUMENT FOR GOD'S EXISTENCE FROM OBJECTIVE MEANING

I will next make what I consider a sound argument for the external existence of God from objective meaning to support a rational faith in Him. Such an argument has not been made previously, as far as I know. My argument is deductive (= only thinking, not observing things which induction does). (See Appendix I on the types of arguments.) The premises of a deduction are assumed true because again it is a process of only thinking, not of observing or experimenting. Each premise must first be critically examined to determine whether or not it is true (= a belief that matches, pictures, represents, or corresponds to in some way a thing of any type, including ideas). The conclusion follows validly or with necessity, not just probability, if all the many laws of deduction are followed.

This argument is based on objective meaning in the universe (= the physical whole or all space and everything in it, including all forms of matter and energy).

The first premise of this deductive argument for God's existence from meaning is that "the universe has objective meaning". I believe that this assumption is totally reasonable common sense because everything has some effect on what it relates to whether or not any human knows it. (See Section 2 on the definition of "meaning" as "significant impact.")

The second premise of this argument is that, "God created the universe." I will show that this premise is true in Section 27, #1 on the creator argument for God's existence.

The conclusion follows validly that, "Therefore, God's existence has objective meaning."

I maintain that this argument provides the evidence necessary for a rational faith in an objective or external God. In other words, I consider the argument from objective meaning a plausible and strong reason for such a faith.

TWO IMPLICATIONS follow from this argument for God from meaning:

1. The first is that *God is sheer meaning itself* (in all the senses of meaning, especially the "ultimate significance" of everything because He is their creator), not that He is in everything. *God Himself is thus strictly spiritual. Further, He is the source of all great values* such as goodness, love, and truth. (See Section 3, #4 on how meaning encompasses all values.) *These values in themselves, not as we incompletely know and embody them, are also (like God) sheerly meaningful in that they consist of only positive truths about what has worth in general.*

2. The second implication of the argument from meaning is that *God is the ultimate source of all meaning.* By creating the universe He also created all meaning. There can be no meaning if nothing exists because something's meaning primarily expresses its impact on or relationship to something else.

The creation of meaning obviously requires tremendous power to bring the universe into existence. Recall that the primary definition of "meaning" is "the significant impact of anything." (See Section 2.) Impact comes from power, all of which again ultimately derives from the enormous power or energy needed to create the universe from nothing. (See Sections 40 on the power of intangibles and 27, #1 on the creator argument for God.)

Both of these implications tighten the connection between God and meaning, perhaps too much so, but I cannot pursue them and their criticisms more here according to my common-sense approach. (See Section 8.)

27

THREE MORE ARGUMENTS FOR GOD'S EXISTENCE

I will now very briefly summarize three traditional arguments for the objective or external existence of God to support a rational faith in Him to show that belief in the divine is meaningful (in the sense of "objectively true"): (1) from the creation of the universe, (2) from the grand design (plan) of the universe, and (3) from mysticism or personal experiences of God. *I consider these three arguments sound and meaningful (in the currently required sense of "plausible" or rationally probable) in establishing His external existence.* I have modified these arguments to express what I consider to be their strongest forms from the point of view of meaning. While these three arguments have little to do with meaning itself, they give answers to the God-question which is the most meaningful one that a person can ask, as I have emphasized. Some recent theories of cosmology (study of the universe) such as multiple universes hold that more than one universe exist, but none of these has been demonstrated yet. All these theories are speculation now with reasons to support them but no empirical (concrete) evidence or test them yet.

I emphasize yet again that sound plausible arguments for the external existence of God ought to be what most gives meaning to God and the immortal afterlife.

The Creation of the Universe

1. THE CREATOR OF THE UNIVERSE ARGUMENT maintains that the universe (again, = everything that exists physically) needs God to create it from nothing. Many people think that this is obvious. Yet, the first law of thermodynamics in physics maintains that energy (matter in another form) can neither be created nor destroyed, only transformed into different states. So why cannot all matter or the universe itself always have existed, perhaps in different forms? *We thereby need a strong reason to believe that the universe requires something SUPERnatural (= beyond or superior to or more than all nature or the universe) to make it exist for each sound argument for the objective existence of God.*

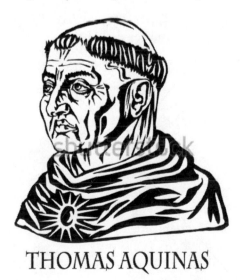

THOMAS AQUINAS

I believe that there is such a reason in the argument for God's existence from a creator, which originated from medieval philosopher Thomas Aquinas in his five "ways" or arguments to know that God exists. His second argument from a creator or first cause of the universe has the first premise that for anything to exist, it must have a cause (= anything that makes an efect),which was several centuries later found to be essential to getting any scientific knowledge.

Aquinas' version of the first cause or creator argument is quite brief. He argued that every effect or thing must be preceded by a cause that makes it exist. Each of these causes must likewise be preceded by a cause that makes it exist. Eventually there must be a first cause that started all the causes. Aquinas called this first cause "God." We need not ask, "What caused God?" because we have arrived at the end of causes that goes beyond nature (or the universe) into the supernatural. There can be no higher cause than that: it is the highest one possible.

It is little noted that not only does a cause precede its effect, but also that *it must be greater than its effect* to make it exist, for example, fire causes wood to be hot. Wood has only the potential to be hot, not its actuality or physical reality as fire has. This premise of the need for a greater cause leads to the conclusion that *there must be a cause greater than all nature or the universe itself. Aquinas wrote that, "We call this first cause God." Further, the first cause must be actual* in order to make the universe's existence actual too.

It is also little noted that Aquinas' argument for a creator or first cause implies that a cause not only precedes but also is "higher" than its effect because it has actual powers that their effects lack as, for example, the actual heat of fire that makes the potential in wood to be hot. Eventually we need to infer that a highest cause exists. This cause must by logical consistency be higher than all nature or the universe: it must be supernatural. Aquinas called it "God." Again, there is no need to ask, "What caused the highest cause?" because there must a starting point to existence. Nothing can be higher than the highest.

Kant severely criticized Aquinas' creator argument by maintaining that causes do not extend beyond the physical world of things and events. This criticism is strong, but it misses a main point of the creator argument that *everything needs some reason greater than itself, not necessarily a cause, to explain why it exists. There must be a greater reason for something to exist, for example, humans with minds are required to make a manufactured thing such as a car. For the universe this reason can only be the intangible of God.* If we again carry this premise to its completion, *we validly conclude that the universe needs some reason greater than itself to create it.* This can be only a creator God.

I maintain that this version of the creator argument is another meaningful (in the senses of "strong" and "plausible") one for the objective existence of God in addition to the argument from objective meaning. It shows that we have the sound reasoning of the need for a higher reason to believe that an external God that is supernatural or more than (above or superior to) nature exists to create it.

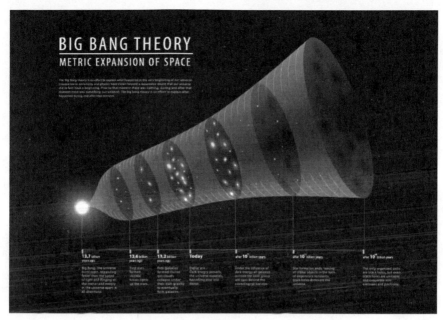

The Big Bang

THE BIG BANG: The argument for God as the creator of the universe has very recently received empirical (experimental or physical) support by the scientific proof that the Big Bang happened. This is (=) the scientific explanation that the universe began with extremely dense matter and high temperature that exploded in the beginning. Its main finding is that *before the Big Bang 13.799 billion years ago, absolutely nothing existed: no matter, no space, and no time. Only God could create the universe from nothing* since that is all that existed before the Big Bang.

Cosmological scientists have proven in 2012 that the Higgs Boson (the elementary particle that gives mass to energy) also physically exists. (See Section 36 for more on the Higgs.) So matter or nature could not exist by itself eternally to account for the universe. *This particle needs to be created by God since it shows that matter did not exist by itself.* Only God could have created the Higgs to make matter exist because we now know that there was nothing before the Big Bang, that is, at the beginning or start of the universe.

Since both the Big Bang and the Higgs Boson have now been proven to exist by scientists, they add *strong support to the creator argument that something supernatural created the universe.* Such evidence gives meaning (in the sense of "physical evidence") to the objective existence of God.

God creating the universe according to Bernini

From the point of view of meaning, *because God is the tremendous power that created the universe, He should properly be called "the Power of Meaning" or its "Force."* (See Section 40 on the power of intangibles.) This Power or Force is an infinitely creative one rather than a natural one. (Praying to God for something may well not get it because this blackmails or extorts Him.)

This last term recalls the final words of the first *Star Wars* (1977) movie, "May the Force be with you." Filmmaker George Lucas stated to broadcast journalist Charlie Rose that he made the concrete metaphor of the Force from the world religions, especially eastern ones such as Taoism. The Force tells Luke Skywalker that his life will be highly meaningful. The seven other films in this saga tell about how he struggles to hold on to his faith in the mystical energies of the Force in the face of cosmic threats such as the Death Star.

2. THE GRAND DESIGN (PLAN) ARGUMENT maintains that *the design of the universe, especially the earth, is so complex that it requires a divine designer or planner. This argument does not maintain that the universe needs a supernatural creator, although it does not deny it.* A design is (=) anything planned for a purpose. Purpose is one of the four main senses of the word "meaning" (in Section 3) and one of the most spiritual words.

An example of a design that scientists cannot explain is the fact that species of animals have the purpose of striving to survive. Who can doubt that the earth and the universe have grand designs, from the smallest (such as amazing subatomic particles, cells, and genes) to the largest (such as the billions of galaxies and trillions of stars?(See Section 30 on the vastness of the universe.)

Current science, especially the biological theory of evolution, can now account well for HOW these grand designs evolved on earth. Yet, it cannot explain WHY this grand design exists. Only a divine designer can explain why the earth is so fine-tuned that it has such amazing, complex, and intelligent life as humans for whom it seems designed. (This version of the argument is currently called the "anthropic principle.") There must be an answer to the question why *species of animals and plants are so well designed that they have the goal of survival. Lacking higher consciousness, they cannot give a purpose to themselves.*

Finally, *when we experience the grand designs in the world (earth) and the universe, we can feel awe (*amazement touched with fear of a higher power like God). This emotion of awe is more than wonder which is what nature would evoke. Therefore, the design argument provides yet still another strong and plausible argument (reason) to believe that a supernatural God objectively exists because His existence alone answers the ultimate "Why?" question regarding the existence of grand plan or design of the earth.

3. THE MYSTICAL (PERSONAL) EXPERIENCES ARGUMENT comes from experiences which are (=) *personal encounters with or feelings of the presence of God. Many people claim that they have had an experience of the divine, many of them in totally convincing ways to themselves.* Didn't Moses talk to God and then he freed the Hebrews from slavery in Egypt by many miracles, or are these just stories? Didn't apostle Paul encounter Him on the road to Damascus? That experience completely changed his life and much of the history of Christianity.

Millions of people in both the eastern and western hemispheres are likewise strongly convinced that they have experienced God in such places as prayer, church, nature, doing advanced yoga, and other areas that predispose a person to experience God. As artist Frederick Franck wrote, "Authentic spirituality is intimately connected to firsthand, direct experiencing" (*What Matters, page 12*).

I myself have not had a mystical experience, but *there needs to be only one genuine case of a person who has actually experienced God to verify that He exists.* Surely those millions who strongly affirm that they have experienced God personally cannot all be deluded or mistaken. Therefore, the argument from mystical experiences provides a final strong and plausible reason to support a rational faith that a supernatural God externally exists in addition to the arguments from objective meaning for God, the creator or greatest reason of the universe, and its grand design.

28

WARNINGS ABOUT THE
ARGUMENTS FOR GOD'S EXISTENCE

I warn that *these arguments for God represent only the results of human reasoning (thinking).* Throughout this book I emphasize how limited and weak this is. *All the arguments both for and against God can be criticized to varying degrees as fallacious. (See Appendix I on fallacies.) Nevertheless, these arguments give us the most that we can know now about the divine. We should follow and believe our reasoning wherever it leads daily throughout our lives to know more about the objective or true meaning (primarily in the fundamental sense of "existence") of God. We can always know more truths about God and His existence, but never the full truth because that is too much for humans to know.* (See Section 70 on this view of truth.)

To repeat for emphasis (Section 25): If God's existence were obvious, our lives would clearly have the obvious meaning (in the sense of "purpose") to totally love and serve Him because the great reward of an eternal afterlife of bliss awaits everyone who does this. Yet,*neither God's existence nor our purpose is obvious at all.* Since so much is at stake in the God-question (possible immortal joy), we all must be sure that we try to determine the objective meaning of this question as best that we can on an (almost) daily basis, always realizing how weak we are on this.

To emphasize again: *as is true for all the big questions about intangibles, humans can never know all the truths about God, including His existence* and nature (traits, for examples, goodness, power and perfection), with our very finite intellects. I think that it is more likely by far that a *person can always get more higher truths about whether or not God exists.* (See Section 70.) These broadening truths may argue for either God's existence or His non-existence, but they are "higher" if they give us more clarity about and insight into the many extremely complex and abstract issues in the God-question.

29

ARGUMENTS AGAINST GOD'S EXISTENCE: THE PROBLEM OF EVIL

We next need to briefly consider the main arguments against or "disproving" God's existence to decide whether or not He externally exists so that our answer to the God-question examines both its sides. Again, much meaning, namely, our eternal afterlife of joy, is at stake in the God-question. (See Section 25.) Affirmatively answering the arguments against God's external existence should logically result in atheism (= the belief that no God truly exists) which implies that we all would have only one short bittersweet life on earth—with its emphasis on the sweet!

It is often said that God's existence cannot be disproven because "it is impossible to prove a negative, namely, that He does not exist: there may be a proof of God that we simply do not know about. This is a huge problem for any argument that attempts to prove that something does not exist.

The strongest traditional argument against God's existence is from evil (= undeserved suffering). Why would an all-good, all-loving, and all-powerful God allow so much evil? There is certainly far more evil than we would expect from such a God, for examples, lovers betraying each other, frequent brutal wars, murder and starvation of millions of people (by dictators Stalin and Mao, for examples), racial prejudice, and the death of young children (novelist Fyodor Dostoevsky's most troubling example—what's yours?).

In view of so much evil, every believer in God needs to have a convincing theodicy (= defense of God's goodness in view of evil). The most popular one is that so much evil results from the great good of human free will or choice to do evil actions. Not God, but human free choices cause the horrendous evils that we witness, asserts this theodicy. It also asserts that humans are better and blessed if they are free rather than caused to do their actions. (See Section 45 on the meaning of free will.)

The free-will theodicy has many severe criticisms, for examples, too much evil results (Dostoevsky again, in his novel *The Brothers Karamazov*) and God as a loving Father does not guide and console us enough about so many evils.

I myself agree with these criticisms of the free-will theodicy. *I prefer the theodicy that God is too limited in His power to overcome all evil.* Evil is the ultimate form of meaninglessness. Perhaps it cannot be eliminated even by God, as Plato puzzled in his dialogue "Euthyphro." God may well be working to lessen all evil, but He cannot totally do so now at least. I realize that *such a limited God is far from the traditional conception of Him as perfect in all ways*, but I think that the theodicy of God limited in His power to eliminate evil best explains the meaning of so much evil.

Perhaps God cannot eliminate all evil because it is the fundamental form of meaninglessness (including the sense of "no existence"). This threatens all meaning. Also perhaps God can eventually eliminate all evil, as Zoroaster held at the start of human thinking about God, whom he called "Ahura Mazda."

The problem of evil is among the knottiest in all philosophy. I surely cannot unravel its complexities and intricacies here according to my common sense approach (in Section 8). I now need to move to the next argument against God's existence.

The Andromeda Galaxy

30

ARGUMENTS AGAINST GOD II: THE VAST UNIVERSE

The argument from the vastness of the universe is the newest one against the existence of God. This argument maintains that since the universe has recently been discovered to be unimaginably huge, literally with billions of galaxies with some giants having one hundred trillion (one million million) stars, it is quite hard to believe that God could care about one person on the tiny earth. All of this has been proven to be still expanding—but into what? Empty space? That is still something. It cannot expand into God because He is an intangible and so takes up no space. Can the newly discovered (starting with the Hubble Telescope about 1990) vastness of the universe show God's glory in His love of so many galaxies? Possibly, but this surely strains the conception of even a perfect God!

The Big Bang now tells us that the universe is finite in time and space, in fact, it is accelerating at a faster pace. (See Section 27 on the Big Bang.) The vastness of the universe differs tremendously from the early Christian theology of the earth-centered universe, which the Christian church based its theology for many centuries and still seems to imply in the popular oversimplified view that persists, for example, for a person to pray to God to get a favor. *The vast universe now seems to many people very natural, empty, cold, and purposeless (pointless). (See Section 54 on nihilism.)*

Most people today have much difficulty in conceiving anything as real except physical things. Proving that something more than the physical exists is perhaps the hardest task in all philosophy today, as in the arguments for intangibles. (See Section 36.) More and more people are now favoring metaphysical materialism (defined as the "belief that matter is the only reality" in Section 33). This materialism now seems rather obvious to atheists, although most of them rarely think about the God-question. *Materialists find insufficient evidence for God's existence—because they accept only physical proof!* (See next section.)

We still have so much to know about the universe such as dark matter and dark energy. These comprise approximately ninety-five per cent of it. The recent argument against the existence of God from the vastness of the universe accords well with the amazing new discoveries about it.

31

ANSWERING AGNOSTICS

Agnostics emphasize how extremely hard that it is to know, especially with today's strictly scientific (factual) way of knowing, the correct answer to the God-question. An agnostic neither affirms nor denies God's existence. She claims only that (=) "we cannot know whether or not God truly exists." Agnosticism is definitely a main reason that people today do not believe in God. When presented with an argument for God's existence, an agnostic always responds, "We cannot know." By "know," she means "know only by means of physical proof," of course.

In practice agnostics are atheists because they live as if God does not exist. They tend not to ask the God-question since they are convinced that they cannot know its correct answer. Can this change? Only if an *agnostic develops her theory of knowledge directly on whether or not she can know that intangible truths like an external God exist.* This theory would be complex, abstract, and difficult. Almost everyone, including almost all agnostics, would have no clue how to even start to construct it. Today's agnostic implicit theory of knowledge, called "empiricism," insists that we can know truths only about physical things that we can experience and ideas strictly derived from these.

What an agnostic really needs to do is to think hard about whether or not we can know anything, especially intangibles like God, that we cannot experience physically. Very few agnostics do this. They tend to insist on saying, "We cannot know" whenever nonphysical considerations are introduced into an argument for God's existence. Yet, they need to explain how we can know only by our physical experiences such intangible and totally abstract truths as advanced mathematics and even arithmetic (big numbers), logical laws (such as identity or A = A), scientific laws especially in physics and all values such as goodness, justice and beauty.

Agnostics seem content to find out the true answer to the God-question at their deaths. Then, as Socrates first said in his *Apology* for a different purpose (to provoke thinking), either there will be nothing of a person, not even blackness, or God does exist and will grant her an immortal afterlife. In the second case, agnostics are convinced that God will accept their inability to know as a justification to admit them to the eternal afterlife of blessedness as long as they have lived a good life by at least not hurting others. They basically believe that their inability to know God's existence will not exclude them from heaven. So, they feel secure to find out whether or not God exists after they die. In effect, *agnostics have blind faith in their inability to know whether or not God exists.*

CRITICISMS: Many agnostics believe that not much is at stake in the God-question, but they are quite mistaken about this. (See Section 26.) If the traditional God (and the afterlife) truly exists, He will not reward agnostics unless they have made an extended effort to know how we know big truths (intangibles) in general and whether or not we can know that an external God exists in particular. (See Section 25.) This view again emphasizes God's justice or fairness rather than His mercy which would allow everyone to enjoy the afterlife despite the efforts that each person makes. Punishment is fair if a person knowingly violates divine rules, no? Agnostics tend to be disdainful toward the God-question. They rarely even mention the crucial knowledge-question.

CONCLUSIONS ABOUT GOD AND MEANING: *The reader now needs to carefully consider the agnostic's unknowing and the atheist's arguments against God's existence (from the problem of evil and from the vastness of the universe) before she decides what is the meaning of God (in the fundamental sense of His "existence"). Yet still again, a tremendous amount of meaning is at stake in the God-question: the possibility of an immortal afterlife of bliss.* (See Section 25.) We cannot afford to wait, as agnostics do, until after we die to find out the answer to this question because then it would be too late to show a sincere interest in God for His sake. *Taking a "wait-and-see" view toward God's existence will surely result in an agnostic's huge disappointment if He does exist! Agnostics will protest that they acted on what they knew most—very little! They will likely get the divine reply that they did not try hard to be honest with themselves about the urgency of the God-question and inquiring whether or not we can know answers to questions about intangibles such as whether or not God externally exists (the truth-question applied to God).*

In general, each person needs to decide as objectively as she can whether or not God's external existence is meaningful (in the sense of "rationally plausible") and a reasonable faith since we cannot know the whole truth about God. (See Section 70 on this view of broadening truth.)

The answers to the God-question are too complex to have a single meaning for everyone. So God's meaning is more like a lifelong journey that each person ought to take. This pilgrimage to an unknown destination has too much meaning ever to be forsaken. It should turn one's life into a constant seeking and re-examining of the ultimate meaning of our lives: is it our everlasting joy with our loved ones or will we be nothing after our deaths?

32

MY SEEKING GOD

I myself have intensely sought the soundest answer to the God-question since my early teenage years. Like many other seekers throughout history, I have not found much about its answer that is definite or certain. I have found four meaningful (yet still again in the senses of "strong" and "plausible") arguments for God's existence that I have summarized in this part: from objective meaning, the creation of the universe or its greatest reason, its grand design, and mystical experiences of God). These are enough for me to affirm belief in God, although He is now at least limited in power to eliminate evil (negative meaninglessness of death or nonexistence). I think that my position follows the idea of meaning, but this is the most complex question of all.

I was strictly raised as a Roman Catholic, but I do not now practice any religion because I do not find rituals meaningful, even emotionally (subjectively). *I believe in some meaningful ideas from each of the world's major religions. All these religions capture some—never all—intangible truths about God.*

Most briefly, my main conclusions about the objectively most meaningful or intangible truths found in each of the world religions, which were formerly called "comparative religions," are the following: Christianity conceives of a loving creator God; Judaism offers evolving covenants (agreements) from God which express His historical relationships to us; the most meaningful insight of Islam is that every person owes absolute submission to God as the supreme being (BUT ONLY IF God can be known to exist which Islam tends to ignore today).

The most meaningful truth in Hinduism is that we can feel truly united with God after rigorously practicing mental types of yoga. Finally, Buddhism fundamentally holds the meaningful truth that we should enjoy but not be attached to this world of suffering by being a separate self. Buddha himself insisted on the courageous but extreme view the self should be totally obliterated in Nirvana or all that exists.

For a fuller treatment of the specific truths that I find meaningful in each world religion, please see Issue #62 of my *Meaning of Life* journal, pages 10–13 available from me at seekerofmeaning@yahoo.com.

Symbols of the world religions

I am not sure about whether or not an afterlife awaits me. There are too many questions about the notion of my eternal joy with God and my loved ones; for examples, what if one of my loved ones does not get into heaven or what if I do not? I do not have enough knowledge to answer such extremely speculative questions. Like many thinkers, *my search for God has been tormenting* because so much meaning is at stake and I have limited, but increasing or broadening, knowledge. (See Section 70 on this view that of truth.)

PART IV

MATERIALISM AND INTANGIBLES

33

SOURCE OF MEANING #7: MATERIAL POSSESSIONS

This source is almost the opposite of seeking God because it is wholly physical whereas God is totally abstract or intangible. It is far and away *the main source in the daily lives for the vast majority of people today* because they make sure that they first of all survive by providing food, shelter, clothing, and the like for themselves. We cannot not have this source if we are to simply survive.

Another reason for the popularity of this source is that the meaning of a thing is physical and usually simple. It takes no imagination to appreciate things. *To have or own things becomes the first, biggest, simplest, and most urgent goal of most people today.*

Possessions are an enormous temptation that ensnares multitudes of people as their primary source of meaning. Much of our time is devoted to only this source in the forms of work and shopping which compose the main means to it. We get immediate concrete rewards from it. So, many people today think that having many material possessions gives their lives most meaning over even quality relationships and seeking God.

I call the philosophy that "material possessions are the main meaning of life" (=) *materialism,* but not the metaphysical sense (= only matter exists). Let us call this philosophy "ethical materialism" because it maintains that owning material possessions is the greatest good of one's life. *Possessions are the easiest source of meaning to get,* usually requiring only some money.

These benefits give it tremendous appeal over all the other sources. As business magnate Armand Hammer once stated, "Money is my first, last and only love." (quoted by Naylor, Willimon, and Naylor, *The Search for Meaning, page 22*). The other sources can give a person much meaning, but they are quite hard to get, for examples, a sense of community, dialogue, art, seeking God and intangibles. Whew! These sources are loads of work! Also, they are hard for many people to appreciate and even know.

34

CRITICISMS OF MATERIALISM

A person pays a high price for the easy and obvious meaning of possessions. In themselves they have only a little meaning, mostly just enabling physical survival. The bigger that they are (such as houses, boats, and money) the more meaning that they have. Yet, most things are not large.

A possession does not much affect the quality of our lives or their prosperity. Recent scientific studies show that people are happy when they buy something typically for approximately one hour. People in poor countries often have closer relationships to others than in affluent ones like the U. S. This gives to the poor people more meaning than owning things does to the wealthy.

We can easily become so enslaved to the consumption of things. Materialism can easily blind us to the higher sources of meaning, for examples, community and dialogue. Because this source is limited to physical things, it is almost fatal to a full life of meaning that we can get from the other sources such as intangibles. (See Section 35.)

We *need to connect materialism to broader sources,* for examples, improving relationships and finding fulfilling work. *Money itself is a good means because it keeps us from bartering and physically fighting for things themselves, but it ought never be an end or goal in itself.*

How meaningful is materialism? Not much. It often does not have a big impact, on the quality of life of a person other than survival only for more of the same.

Possessions do not fulfill the high human needs, for examples, the intellectual and the spiritual. Things are quite dense to thinking. *Pursuing only material things is obviously quite shallow.* Who wants the meaning of their life to be only that? The media, especially television, conditions us to be only consumers. Possessions can furnish anyone a safe but mindless harbor of slight meaning in our stormy sea of uncertainty about the other sources.

Today people passionately pursue materialism. We often dignify our quest for it such as buying furniture, adding to one's house or taking a vacation to an amusement park by calling them our "dreams." *We desperately need viable alternatives to materialism. Such alternatives* can *come from all the other sources of meaning,* particularly quality relationships, community, dialogue, fulfilling work and art. How sad that so many people prefer materialism!

I myself have had little use for materialism. I worked most of my life for exploitive wages as an adjunct (teaching part-time at one college, but in other colleges during the same semester) commuting long distances to nineteen colleges in my career. Yet, I and my family lived in our own lovely single-family houses with large yards in Chicago near many arts, museums and cultural events. My children went to expensive private schools instead of the bad public ones. So even though I have disregarded materialism, I have lived somewhat prosperously nevertheless. Thinking about and making meaning gives me greater joy by far than materialism could.

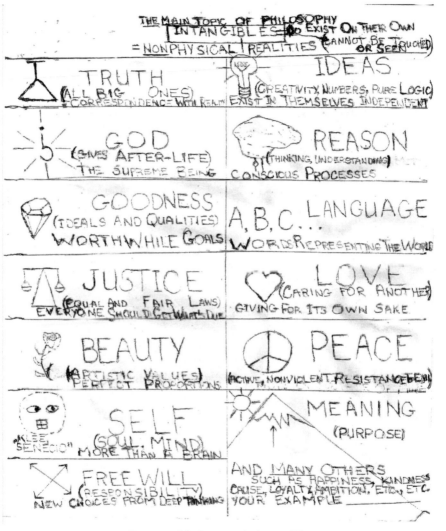

THE MAIN TOPIC OF PHILOSOPHY
INTANGIBLES = GOD EXIST ON THEIR OWN
= NONPHYSICAL REALITIES (CANNOT BE TOUCHED OR SEEN)

TRUTH
(ALL BIG ONES)
= CORRESPONDENCE WITH REALITY

IDEAS
(CREATIVITY, NUMBERS, PURE LOGIC)
EXIST IN THEMSELVES INDEPENDENT

GOD
(GIVES AFTER-LIFE)
THE SUPREME BEING

REASON
(THINKING, UNDERSTANDING)
CONSCIOUS PROCESSES

GOODNESS
(IDEALS AND QUALITIES)
WORTHWHILE GOALS

A, B, C... LANGUAGE
WORDS REPRESENTING THE WORLD

JUSTICE
(EQUAL AND FAIR LAWS)
EVERYONE SHOULD GET WHAT'S DUE

LOVE
(CARING FOR ANOTHER)
GIVING FOR ITS OWN SAKE

BEAUTY
(ARTISTIC VALUES)
PERFECT PROPORTIONS

PEACE
(ACTIVE, NONVIOLENT RESISTANCE TO EVIL)

"KLEE SENECIO" SELF
(SOUL, MIND)
MORE THAN A BRAIN

MEANING
(PURPOSE)

FREE WILL
(RESPONSIBILITY)
NEW CHOICES FROM DEEP THINKING

AND MANY OTHERS
SUCH AS HAPPINESS, KINDNESS
CAUSE, LOYALTY, AMBITION, ETC., ETC.
YOUR EXAMPLE

Diagram #2: Some main intangibles

35

SOURCE #8: INTANGIBLES, POTENTIALLY THE BIGGEST

*T*he hardest source of meaning to know but potentially the largest is the nonphysical source that I call the "intangibles." This word denotes that *they cannot be touched, but they also cannot be seen* since they are not concrete things. Intangibles are metaphysical or *beyond the physical on another level of existence.* We cannot weigh or measure them in any way. If we could, we would easily answer all life's big questions by favoring the heaviest or biggest intangible in each case! However, *the embodiment of an intangible in a person does have degrees of more/ less or lower/higher.* So, it is correct in these cases to talk about "more" or "less" meaning.

I define "*intangibles*" *as* (=) "*immaterial realities.*" *They consist of (1) the greatest values (for examples, goodness, beauty, love, and justice) and (2) the greatest ideas (for examples, the self, God, and free will).* (See Diagram #2.)

I maintain that *intangibles are mostly objective* (= existing external to or independent of our minds), as they were originally conceived before modern western philosophers became highly subjective. Intangibles are subjective only in such respects as we know and believe them. (See Part VI, especially Section 48 on subjective and objective meaning.)

Similarly, Plato's Ideas are primarily objective truths and values. For him, the proper answers to all the big questions of life consist of knowing the geometrical harmonies and proper proportions. (See examples of Plato on beauty in Section 24. the just community in Section 16 and a healthy individual in Section 62. (Again, I capitalize "Ideas" for Plato because they differ much from the current view and usage of "ideas" as totally subjective thoughts.)

The meaning that we can get from knowing an intangible truth is unlimited. Surely, the *knowledge of all intangible truths is not given to humans.* A person can know one intangible truth at a time at best by means of an extended intellectual effort. (See Section 38 on intuition of intangible truths.) Since intangibles transcend (go beyond) the physical world, they cannot be known by our senses, only by our minds. Then we can apply them with much benefit to our daily decisions. For a general example, if a person knows a truth from the intangible of goodness for a personal ethical problem, she can apply it to do a good act that solves it. Knowing intangibles thus can give a person truths that she needs to live the most meaningful life that she can.

Our chief problem with intangibles is knowing intangible truths.

The following are examples of intangible truths from several intangibles (indicated in boldface):

GOODNESS: A good action is one that you are willing to do to anyone, including yourself. (Kant's categorical imperative or the Golden Rule which is found in all world religions).

An innocent human has intrinsic value (worth in itself and for its own sake). (Ethics tells us to follow such truths, but very sadly it cannot force us to do so.)

FREE WILL: A person can make a free choice by thinking of a new idea, to her, that she was not caused to think and that gives her an option that she can choose. (See Sections 46 and 47 for a fuller treatment and examples of free will.)

BEAUTY: Beauty consists of the proper proportions of the geometric forms of an object (from Plato—see Section 24).

Some aspects of your favorite artworks ought to be (prescriptive) fascinating for you just to perceive (from Kant--see Section 21 on disinterest).

These examples show overall that intangible truths tell us a little about the meaning of life. Their main message seems, to me, to be that *we are on earth to do more than buy possessions; instead we are to thrive (flourish or prosper) and to find fulfillment in ourselves and with others, by ideally at least implicitly knowing and then applying intangible truths. I I believe that his best answers the question why we exist from the point of view of intangibles.*

36

SIX ARGUMENTS FOR THE EXISTENCE OF INTANGIBLES

Since intangibles are an extremely important but controversial and difficult source of meaning, *we must be very sure that they actually exist obectively or externally to our knowing minds.* I will now present, as briefly as I can, six arguments for the existence of intangibles. These arguments need to show that intangibles exist independently of us, not as mere abstractions that we make up from sense data in our brains. Intangibles obviously offer much more meaning than materialism: they can make much meaning by answering our deepest questions about values such as goodness and justice and solving our biggest problems.

As in the arguments for and against God's existence (Sections 25–32), the reader needs to decide for herself how strong the arguments for intangibles are overall by reasoning (thinking) in accord with the laws of logic. This is the best method that humans have to know the greatest truths, even if it is not simple or even definite. Alas! (See Appendix I.)

Since the arguments for intangibles are so abstract and hard to understand, the reader may want to skip reading them, even though beliefs supported by logical arguments have much more meaning, as for God.

1. THE ARGUMENT FROM HIGHER LEVELS OF EXISTENCE maintains that *existence overall has progressive gradations that culminate in the intangibles.* As Plato and many other thinkers have argued, reality consists of a "great chain of being" (existence). This chain orders all reality. Every link in it must be filled or it is broken. Its hierarchy ranges from the lowest kinds of things, such as dirt and minerals, on the bottom. The middle levels of the spectrum consist of plants and animals. Intangibles such as justice, beauty, and goodness make up the higher links in the great chain. As God embodies all the intangibles (Section 26), He is the highest link. Just like all the other links, intangibles are thus required to exist objectively by the great chain of being (existence).

Recall here that the creator argument for God's existence shows that everything needs something greater than itself to make it exist. (See Section 27, #1.)

2. HUMAN CONSCIOUSNESS *(= a person's internal awareness of anything.* This includes self-consciousness or you being aware that you yourself are aware of being aware or, in other words, that you are aware that it is you who are aware!) *consists solely of our states of mind, not any tangible thing itself. It is strictly subjective, inner, and private whereas things are totally objective, external to us and public.* Our brains cannot be conscious because they consist only of—soggy! sponge-like! gooey!—material cells. How can such slimy stuff be aware of itself? The human brain has far too few electrical sparks (about 40 watts) to become conscious and thinking which very probably does not come from electricity anyhow. To be sure, *a person needs a functional brain to be conscious of anything, but that is not enough (sufficient) by itself.* She needs the intangible of consciousness to make the brain aware or conscious.

Tangible things have color, shape, location, weight, and size. Consciousness does not have any of these, although it can be aware of all of them. So consciousness differs tremendously from physical or tangible things. How can it come only from our brains? Where or how can consciousness, including thinking, and the brain meet and interact? No one has explained how consciousness can exist except as an intangible. Experimental psychologists after many years of trying hard have explained how the brain can explain only lower-level phenomena such as pain and memory, but certainly not higher ones such as thinking, imagining, creativity, and consciousness itself.

Please re-read Section 5 on the inner voice as another argument for intangibles from consciousness. How can the marvelous and wonderful inner voice and ear be explained by one's gooey brain?

PLATO'S ALLEGORY OF THE CAVE

2. THE WORLD OF EXTERNAL IDEAS (INVISIBLE WORLD)
OR REALM

BEAUTY   JUSTICE   LOVE   MEANING   THE GOOD

ONE GETS KNOWLEDGE OF INTANGIBLES

TRUTH   FREE WILL   SOUL (SELF)

1. THE WORLD OF THE SENSES
(THE VISIBLE WORLD)

THE FIRE "WEAKLY" REFLECTS THE SUN

ONE LEARNS TO "SEE" OTHER REALITIES

PRISONERS OF THEIR SENSES

BREAKS CHAINS ESCAPES

ESCAPED PRISONER

MUST RETURN

SIDE VIEW OF THE CAVE

FRONT VIEW OF CAVE

(SEE VELASQUEZ; PHILOSOPHY, PAGES 4-6)

Diagram #3: Plato's allegory of the cave

3. INTANGIBLE TRUTHS GIVE US GREATER KNOWLEDGE.

Knowledge from tangible things cannot give us truths about intangibles. All our sensing does not give us, for example, what is ethically good. Such truths are not labeled or stamped or even derived from anything physical that we experience. There must thus be an intangible idea of goodness (the good) in order for us to know which actions are morally right (good) and wrong (bad).

Plato in his "allegory (a story in which things symbolize ideas) of the cave" illustrated how it is as if we all are imprisoned in a very imperfect dark cave, but there we have some perfect knowledge, for examples, in arithmetic, algebra, and geometry. (See Diagram 2 for his cave in general.)We know about the perfect triangle such as its angles, even though it does not exist in physical reality. Plato argued that this knowledge can come only from external Ideas (yet again, capitalized because he argued that they exist objectively). So even in the cave of earth we can know Platonic Ideas such as triangles and numbers on which we can construct the axioms (fundamental principles) for branches of mathematics. Prisoners in the cave know by their senses such as sight only what Plato called "weak reflections" of reality. They can know the big truths with their minds with much difficulty after they escape from the cave of their senses.

Humans always fall far short in knowing intangibles, but *at least we have come to know increasingly more intangible truths.* For example, starting with the physics of Aristotle then to Newton and now to Einstein, over the centuries we have come to know more by far about the truths of the physical universe and more comprehensive theories about them. To do this, these scientists know more and more intangible truths in fields such as physics time space, and mathematics.

For another example, because of knowing some intangible truths of ethics such as the equality in dignity of all humans we have become more moral today than less than two centuries ago when almost everyone believed that slavery and the genocides of native people are ethical.

Yet another example: the development of intangible ideas about symbolic logic in the twentieth century made deduction far more complete than in Aristotle's traditional logic which extends only to combinations of simple sentences. (See Appendix I on deduction.)

For example yet again: if a person knows an intangible truth of justice, she can treat other people more fairly.

I conclude from these examples that we can know *more by means of intangibles truths in all fields of study* in addition to the above illustrations from science, ethics, deduction, and justice.

4. OUR KNOWING IS PARTIALY INTANGIBLE. We get much knowledge from our senses, particularly seeing. Yet, *sensory experience does not give us knowledge until we make a conscious (which is itself intangible, see argument #2) judgment about what we sensed. Also, we need to interpret all our sense data in terms of intangible ideas to categorize or classify them,* as Kant argued to an extreme degree in his *Critique of Pure Reason.* For example, when we see a group of people, we instantly categorize them as "humans." Our minds thus impose these categorizing ideas on our sense data in order for us to know them in an abstract way, that is, in our minds. This argument provides additional reasons and support that our minds are more than our brains. (See again argument #2 from consciousness for intangibles.)

Another way to express this argument is that *we do not get knowledge from our sensory experiences of the world until we make a judgment about them.* Metaphorical ways of expressing this argument are that we must "grasp" or "get" with intangible ideas our sensations that we get from experiencing the world before we can know anything about it.

The faculty of judgment is neither tangible nor found in our brains. Only after a person understands her sensations can she get knowledge of them. One's understanding does this instantly. So we need the intangibles of consciousness and the understanding to get knowledge.

Current studies in genetics so far tend to confirm that we are "wired" to know and understand intangible truths. These studies are confirming that we have innate capacities of knowing. For example, political philosopher Noam Chomsky (when he was a linguist) argued that all humans are born with the capacity to learn a language. He revived in a very different way philosopher Rene Descartes' argument that we all are born with "innate ideas"—today he would have called them "inborn truths." At the least we have innate capacities, inclinations or tendencies, as philosopher Wilhelm Leibniz criticized him, for examples, to learn a language (Chomsky), to learn in general, and to understand ("grasp") intangible truths such as Descartes' "I think, therefore I am" which maintains that humans cannot doubt that they are thinking because doubt is itself a type of thinking.

5. WE HAVE INTANGIBLE CONSTRAINTS ON OUR BEHAVIOR. *Something intangible in humans makes it wrong for us to do clearly unethical actions,* for example, poking an innocent friend in the eye. Doing such actions would violate the dignity of the other, the respect that we owe her, and ethical goodness, all of which are intangibles. In general, we are constrained from committing clearly immoral actions such as cheating, stealing, and murder. "Constraints" can be defined as (=) "limitations on our behaviors imposed by the intangibles of goodness and justice."

We likewise have constraints on treating people wrongly on the social level as well as the individual one. Constraints apply to all humans since we all have intangible selves. For example, we are not constrained from building a nuclear power plant on Three Mile Island, but we are strictly constrained to treat anyone who was contaminated by nuclear radiation that escaped from there.

Another way of expressing the idea of constraints is that we are ethically obligated to treat a person with the respect that she deserves. An "obligation" is the positive opposite of a constraint. Obligations are intangible duties owed by one person to another, for example, a child owes some gratitude and obedience to her parents.

Our morals are more by far than what our society teaches its children about them which is very little except by the example of our behavior. In Nazi youth camps, young boys were indoctrinated to be Nazis, but some of them rebelled against such teachings as overly-aggressive, racist, inhumane, and indecent, although they did not use these words, of course. Thus, there is something intangible within us, perhaps genetically as in argument #4, that constrains us from doing major immoral actions and obligates us to do major moral ones. Common sense is quite capable of telling us which actions are "major," for example, cheating, stealing, and murdering, although this is difficult for borderline cases.

This argument from constraints comes from my bright colleague and friend for over thirty years, Michael M. Kazanjian.

6. INTANGIBLES EXIST ACCORDING TO CURRENT PHYSICS. I will be quite brief on this argument because it requires knowledge of advanced physics. *It rewards us with physical intangibles,* as paradoxical (seemingly contradictory) as this phrase sounds.

1. *The simplest example of a physical intangible is the photon which is the scientific name for the light particle or light. This has energy, but no mass.* Energy is intangible in some of its aspects. (See Section 40.)

2. Billions of subatomic particles called "neutrinos" have now been proven by current physics at every moment to pass through the earth as if it were empty space. Neutrinos must exist in a different kind of space and they obey different laws. Are they not thereby existing intangibles?

3. The Higgs Boson (popularly but wrongly known as "the God Particle") gives mass. In 2012 the Large Hadron Collider in France and Switzerland proved that it physically exists. The Higgs is yet still another intangible that current physics has proven to exist. (See Section 27 for more on the Higgs.)

4. Now accepted by some notable physicists, the theory of vibrating *superstrings* of the universe holds that it has ten to twenty-six dimensions. Since three of these dimensions are space, time, and matter, the others must be totally different types of matter—how can this be?—or intangible ones. These dimensions cannot be tangible because then we could touch (and see) them.

What stronger argument can there be for the existence of intangibles than these actually existing ones (photons, neutrinos, and the Higgs Boson, but not yet superstrings) which have now been proven scientifically by physics? Some other examples of actual intangibles in current physics are frequently fields such as gravitation, space-time, and perhaps dark matter.

I again—see Section 22 on emotions expressed in Beethoven's *Symphony #9*—owe much of this information to discussions with the brilliant science fiction writer D. H. Robinson.

37

HOW WE LIVE MOSTLY
FOR INTANGIBLES

We all live mostly for intangibles, even if we never say this. For example, do we work more for money or self-respect? Obviously the latter which is an intangible. No worker would long endure a job in which her self-respect is lacking too much, but many workers stay at jobs in which they are not paid enough wages.

The most obvious intangible for which people live is God. They often have blind faith simply to believe that their lives and those of their loved ones will have immortal meaning (in the sense of actual "existence") and joy in heaven. (See Section 25 on blind faith.) These people typically rely on God's commands for all their moral decisions, for example, a highly religious woman preferring a lifetime of emotional and financial commitments to an unwanted child over having an abortion which she fears may send her to hell forever.

The following are some other major examples of how we live for intangibles:

The good is not something that a person buys, but such mental qualities as having a satisfied mind and a sense of well-being;

A quality relationship consists of intangibles such as caring, respect, and love of one person for the other, not by how much stuff or money they exchange;

Parents live much of their lives for the love of their children;

Both physical and mental diseases can be cured more by a patient's or client's positive state of mind than by medicine which often merely hides symptoms from the afflicted;

Unjust wars commit mass social murder; they can be prevented by a love of peace or, according to the writer of *War Is a Force That Gives Us Meaning* Chris Hedges, in a "sense of being in love" in our leaders (quoted in *The Life of Meaning*, edited by Bob Abernethy and William Bole, page 22) rather than by huge armies and weapons which have made wars tragedies for literally millions of innocent men and civilians; this example grimly reminds us that *countless people, mostly young men, give their lives in wars for intangibles* such as justice and freedom; most unfortunately, this frequently results from their not knowing correct intangible truths of justice and mistaking such truths for national pride, glory, and empires based on greed, power, propaganda and the exploitation of the conquered; and

Nuclear wars can quickly contaminate the entire earth with radioactive fall-out, murdering all humans; they must be totally restrained by the intangible of good will—and fear— in the leaders of the nine countries that now have nukes.

Other examples of dying for intangibles are martyrs for God and those hundreds of thousands (at least) who have died in unjust wars between conflicting religious sects in eastern and western hemispheres.

So, *intangibles have much meaning in our lives, especially at critical times. A human can even be said to live mostly for intangibles, especially the sources of high quality relationships and God, although not explicitly.* They are our greatest source of meaning, even beyond materialism. However, I have emphasized how hard it is to know intangible truths. (See the next section on how a person can know them.)

Without intangibles we would be left with knowledge of only—mostly piddly!—facts and unprovable opinions. Only if intangibles exist, can we know higher truths and values and avoid the narrow confines of ethical and metaphysical materialism.

38

WE KNOW INTANGIBLE TRUTHS BY INTUITIONS

I must now explain at least a little more about the key issue of how we can know intangible truths. It is obviously not simple or easy to get this highest knowledge. To know an intangible truth we need to use the highest way of knowing that we have. This way goes beyond even reason (= humans' abstract thinking ability), which is limited to several simple ideas at a time. Human reasoning tends to shut down from overload after conceiving of a few simple ideas at a time, for example: I went to the store today to buy bread... *We need to comprehend (metaphorically "grasp" or "get") an intangible truth with our power of intuition defined as the (=) "direct knowledge of a truth after much reasoning about it."* This is close to having a flash of insight. An example of an intangible truth known by intuition is that "an innocent person ought (prescriptive) to have much value." (See Section 36 for more examples.)

The most that a person can do to predispose herself for an intuition is to reason (think) hard about an intangible, such as goodness and justice, for example, respectively that it is ethical to help the needy and that it is just to help minorities who have been unfairly discriminated against.

An intuition metaphorically *"sees" an intangible truth in your mind's "eye."* It is associated with, but more than, activity in the creative right side of the brain. We cannot explain intuitions by reason because they are a higher way of knowing than it. Perhaps they draw out knowledge latent or dormant in our minds, as Plato maintained, especially in his *Meno*. In this dialogue he draws out the Pythagorean theorem from an uneducated slave boy simply by asking questions.

Plato maintained that we can best know intangibles or what he called (objective or external) "Ideas" when we "participate" in them. By this expression he meant that our minds must somehow become an organic (living) part of an intangible. Yet, he was never satisfied with this account mostly because it has too many metaphors such as "participate" and "organic" and other problems in epistemology (the philosophy of knowledge) that even he could not solve.

More current views of intuition, primarily Freud's, regard it as *preconscious* (an unconscious idea that can become conscious after much reasoning). Again in metaphorical terms, *an intuition is like a "gut feeling"* after a person reflects much. Business executives, detectives and artists have used such feelings with much, but far from complete, success.

An example of an intuitive thinker is human rights activist Rev. Martin Luther King, Jr. As an extroverted type of thinker, he intuited prominent possibilities such as equality, freedom and nonviolence for African-Americans. He most effectively spread these intuitions oblivious to concern about even his own safety which led to his tragic assassination. Another example of a thinker who worked with very similar intuitions is Mahatma Gandhi who led the revolution to overthrow the British colonialism of India. (See Section 40 for more on Gandhi.)

39

MAKING MEANING TESTS
AN INTUITION

A key question of meaning is how can anyone test whether or not an intuition of an intangible truth is true. I propose that this *test is whether or not an intuited intangible truth makes our lives more meaningful.* In other words, does this truth actually improve the quality of our daily lives? If it does, then it is true. For example, since the intuition that restoring justice to people who have been wrongly hurt makes their lives more meaningful (in the sense of "improves the quality of life"), then it is true.

What tougher test of any idea can there be? Isn't this a more vital test than the many theoretical ones such as coherence (a belief is true if the ideas are consistent with other beliefs) and pragmatism (if a belief is true, it works or has practical results—but not vice versa)? The test of making meaning is simply common sense again which we much need, especially for meaning, even though many philosophers today would disagree about the need for both meaning and common sense (See Section 8.)

It is clearly hazardous to apply this test of an intuition of an intangible truth because it often involves predicting some cases in the future which is fundamentally unknowable. Therefore, we can test most intangible truths only retroactively (in the past) by whether or not they have made our lives more meaningful in general. Also, the test of an intuition of an intangible truth needs to make meaning for many people, not just one person except for totally personal cases.

40

THE POWER OF INTANGIBLES

*S*ome intangible truths have power. Not all of them are lifeless. *Their power comes from energy* which is largely physical, but it does have intangible aspects, for examples, at its extremely fast speeds and its lack of a precise location. Newly discovered but unexplained "dark energy" is likely to consist entirely of a different type of energy, perhaps totally intangible. Newly discovered but unexplained dark matter is also likely to consist of much energy. These two discoveries may make up ninety-five per cent of the universe. (See Section 36, #6.)

As Neoplatonist philosophers, especially Plotinus, would have expressed it, intangible truths "emanate" or "radiate" energy. *We all should try as much as we can to be "in touch" with the emanated energy from intangibles.* Whenever we are, we can do much good and many other great values, for examples, Gandhi and King. They both explicitly testified often that they felt this energy for their basic beliefs. They called it "truth to power." This energy resides in intangibles especially goodness, justice, truth, beauty, the self, peacefulness and love. Even some ideas have power. For example, the idea "turn the page of this book" has the power to make readers turn the page, according to Peter McWilliams in *Life 101.*

Gandhi

Energy connects the intangible to the tangible. Much tangible meaning can be achieved by knowing how to do this, for examples, love in a quality relationship and creating communities as Gandhi and King did on a large scale. We much need these connections because intangibles can give us the most meaning amid so much meaninglessness in our lives. With them we can aim for a life of excellence, not perfection mostly due to our finite abilities, despite philosopher Mortimer Adler's assertion that "complete perfection" is "the end of life," quoted by Hugh Moorhead, editor, *The Meaning of Life According to Our Century's Greatest Writers and Thinkers,* page 10.

On the other hand, we must avoid as much as we can the negative energy of bad and evil on us which results in various forms of meaninglessness, especially negative or lack of meaning, for examples, suffering in general, betrayals, prejudice, malice, inflicting pain, and many others. (See Section 52 on meaninglessness.)

Intangibles are the last of the eight sources of meaning treated in this book. *There are many more sources of meaning,* such as the family (children and parents), communicating, luck—which not many people have much of!—and many others, but I have treated some of the main ones. Covering more sources would make this discussion perhaps endless: we can always find more sources of meaning.

A person does not need to have all the sources, for examples, atheists and agnostics do not have the source of God; materialists do not have intangibles.

Each person makes varying degrees of meaning in her sources. *It is obviously ideal to get as much meaningfulness from all the sources as you can.*

PART V

MORE ON MAKING MEANING

This Part will treat various major aspects of making meaning in general other than its sources.

41

ESCAPING ESCAPES FROM MEANING

Making meaning should be the driving force in people but all human history has shown that this has been far from the case. In fact, this has rarely been even mentioned in most of our history. *The main reason that there has been so little making meaning rests in escapes from it.*

Making meaning promises, but also threatens, much in that a person's life may not have much meaning when it is critically examined. The *meaning-question frightens many people to their core because it directly confronts the very purposes of their existence.* Many people do not even raise this question except for materialism (mostly their careers) and quality relationships (mostly marriage, possible children, and usually a few friends). *People thus flee in large numbers to escapes rather than face the distressing prospect that their lives lack meaning.*

An "escape from meaning" can be defined as (=) "any distraction from thinking about or making meaning." Whenever people say that they are "just killing time"—almost the same as their lives!—they are escaping making meaning. If a person keeps herself mindlessly busy, she is also escaping meaning. Escapes fill up much of even our precious little leisure, or what we commonly call our "free," time.

This view of escapes does not deny the need to relax from making meaning, although it does tend to limit this to what is needed.

Making meaning demands much in that it often requires a big effort to increase it. We need much energy to overcome our deep-seated laziness and limited energy. We also need energy to make meaning (in the sense of "quality of life"). *Virtually everyone today feels stress* (mental strain due to demands on a person), but they often can do little to relieve it.

People escape from meaning for a variety of other reasons. A main one is *the fear that they may lose some or even all the meaning that they now have.* As Dewey asked, once you start criticizing your beliefs, where do you stop? He implied that you ought not stop until you have criticized all your beliefs, even your most cherished ones. It would be hard mental work to replace your basic beliefs. *The possibility of losing meaning is terrifying.* I have seen some people almost panic when I mentioned "meaning" to them!

Yet, another reason for escaping meaning is that many people prefer to stay secure with their beliefs such as materialism and blind faith in a saving God than risk losing them for perhaps nothing in exchange except much hard but fruitless mental work. Yet, this fear is unwarranted. *By seeking meaning, we are always seeking truth which is the ultimate (greatest) good of the human mind,* according to M. Adler in *Six Great Ideas,* page 63. Just asking the meaning-question invariably raises the quality of one's life by making that person a seeker. We all ought to take further risks involved in asking this question because *beliefs that are rational and developed are far more meaningful than those that are not. Often when a person examines her basic beliefs, they are quickly destroyed, but they come back stronger and more meaningful (in the sense of "rational"),* according to Professor Melvin Rader in *Enduring Questions,* page 4.

EXAMPLES *of escapes are legion.* Many of them come from the forms of "killing time:" too much shopping and watching television (especially spectator sports) and the many varieties of computing, especially smartphones; drug abuse (including alcohol) and any form of artificially altering one's consciousness, even drinking one beer to do this. Some people escape by acting mindlessly with others, while other people escape by being alone. A widespread example of an escape for today's youth is constantly playing video games on their smartphones.

Our society hinders us all in making meaning by glorifying escapes, for examples, materialism, liquor, indulging in unhealthy but tasty foods, glorifying professional sports, and many others. *Society, in its near-total neglect of deep meaning, is our biggest enemy and obstacle to making meaning. An overpopulated, shallow society in the many temptations to escapes that it emphasizes does much to squelch an individual from even explicitly seeking meaning. Society thereby does much to squelch an individual's search for their authentic self.*

Escaping from meaning happens on the subconscious level as well as the conscious because it stems from a person's repressed fear of living a life lacking meaning. This type of escape much prevents making meaning, but cannot easily be consciously admitted. *A high price must be paid for subconscious escapes.* Anxiety (indefinite unease and apprehension) results. Much boredom and emptiness also results from subconsciously escaping meaning.

CRITICISMS OF ESCAPES: *Escaping from meaning results in mediocrity. This fact makes escapes evil, not just bad,* because they cause us undeserved suffering from not developing our potentials. Escapes from meaning run away from the depths of life rather than dive deeply into them as making meaning does. *Escapees get childish fun, but meaning-makers experience adult joy and deep happiness.*

Escapees from meaning are almost tragic because they do not live fully. In effect, they imply that their lives are largely insignificant by definition. Escapees abandon *what is most distinctive to humans, namely, making meaning.* They "sell out," as they put it in the '60s, meaning which ought to be the pinnacle of their lives.

Critics of this view will object that typical people cannot avoid escaping meaning because they do not have the intellectual and other abilities to live a life of much meaning. I reply that the *typical person can be logical, insightful, and reasonable. That is all that is required to live a life of much meaning* according to the approach of common sense. (See Section 8.) Typical people have much of this whereas intellectuals tend to lack it.

ESCAPING ESCAPES: Who really wants to escape meaning by "killing time"? *Many people just do not know how to make more meaning than they already have, or they lack interest in much* and the energy to overcome their laziness—often caused by depression. (See Section 43 on developing interests.) *The first step in escaping escapes is to realize in both an intellectual and especially an emotional way what meaning is, can be or ought to be in one's life. Next, one ought to realize in much the same way that she is escaping meaning. A person can come to a realization about both meaning and escapes by thinking deeply or by reading about them.*

Another way to escape escapes consists of realizing that the rewards of making meaning are enormous because a person gets more meaning if again she gives her own reasons for her beliefs and actions. Finally, a person can escape escapes if *she makes meaning in the more physical forms,* for examples, improving relationships, working at a fulfilling job and even by buying possessions—but very briefly for the last one! (See Section 34 on criticisms of materialism.)

These ways are neither easy nor simple, of course, but they tell us a little about how we can avoid, lessen or get out of our escapes from meaning. *All of them will be implemented only when the individual herself decides that she wants to, as for all changes within a self.* (See Section 16, #4, on motivation).

42

ESCAPING MEANING THROUGH BLIND FAITH IN GOD

The biggest escape for the typical person is blind faith in (but often in practice close to indifference to) God. This escape maintains that if you believe in God and do not commit big sins that you do not repent, then you can be happy forever in heaven with your family and friends, not in the eternal flames of hell threatened by Jesus. (See Section 25 on blind faith in God.) Amazingly, this escape is not thought about much despite the amount of time at stake—eternity! Its adherents subjectively get so much consolation for deaths that they do not dare to ask the God-question. *This escape effectively stops thinking about the meaning of their lives since it gives a very easy and highly optimistic answer to the meaning-question.* All wrongs, especially deaths, will be made right in the afterlife. What more can anyone ask for? Clearly, *it is quite hard to beat the eternity-offer of blind faith in God! It beats even materialism's offer of simple and immediate, but limited, meaning!* (See Sections 33 and 34.) Thus, a person can escape much making meaning by having blind faith in a saving God who will grant immortal joy.

CRITICISMS: *Blind faith is most appealing to many people because it offers so much and asks for so little back, but surely this is wrong.* God will certainly expect more thought and effort from a person whom He saves for the eternal afterlife if He is just or fair to other people who have done so. I realize that most people will believe whatever favors and flatters them the most, but I emphasize that *blind faith has strictly subjective meaning.* It does not even ask for any evidence that God truly exists. Giving strong reasons for the objective existence of God and the afterlife gives a person more meaning by far than nagging blind faith. Everyone must be brave enough to take the chance that the correct answer to the God-question may be a flat, "No," not to mention the need to do more than just believe in God. (See Section 25 for more criticisms of blind faith.)

I feel very sad for *people who escape to blind faith in God because many of them delude themselves* to believe without any evidence that they will not die and will live forever in joy with their loved ones. Such a self-delusion is a rather pathetic way to live because it stems from weakness and fear of unpleasant realities. However, we can excuse a person for having blind faith due to being born with a low level of intelligence or receiving a poor education, especially a noncritical one.

Are there any ways to escape from the escape from meaning through blind faith? *Only to have the courage to honestly confront the God-question.* It is strictly up to individuals to overcome their fears of lacking meaning. (See Section 16, #4 on motivation.) This is no easy task, to be sure. *It would be best if a person motivates herself to be brave enough to ask the God-question throughout her life to live by the truth rather than a cowardly self-delusion.* Each person needs to realize that she ought to make meaning from more sources than just the escape of blind faith in God.

43

MAKING MORE MEANING

Most people stop making meaning when they feel that they have enough for themselves. For example, raising a family gives all the meaning that many people need or can handle. Yet, how can they be sure that they are so limited? A person can scarcely have "enough" meaning because *making more meaning makes lives better.* Saying that you already have "enough meaning" is in effect saying that you do not care much about it and thus care about little in general.

The main goal of every human ought to be to live the most meaningful life that she can, not just a meaningful one which everyone's life is, at least in their relationships to their families and friends. (See Sections 1 and 3, #1 on impact.) *Everyone's life can be highly meaningful* because we all can make much meaning for others and ourselves. A person's life would be much diminished if she did not try to make more meaning.

We have only one fast and little life on earth. *Why not make the most of it? We can fault anyone who does not try,* if a person is free to do so. (See Sections 45 and 46 on free will.) *We can ask for no more than that a person try as hard as she can to make more meaning.* It is rarely easy to do, as it often requires much effort and depends on others. *I can thereby offer no simple way to make more meaning except to improve all your sources of meaning, even getting more possessions. (See Section 34.) I have described many ways in which a person can do this in my accounts the sources of meaning and my making meaning. (See Section 1 for a list of these sections.)*

Our lives rest on the assumption that they have meaning. A person is never rational in rejecting this assumption. People may think that they are being rational when they reject it—and many other beliefs!—but they are usually motivated by their emotions, usually fear that they can make little or even no meaning. (See Sections 5 on suicide and 41 on subconscious escapes.) If a person stops making meaning, she would stop any special significance that her life can have. (See Section 3, #2 on significance.)

I myself have tried very hard to maximize meaning primarily by developing the idea of meaning and communicating it to as many people as I can. I have also tried to maximize all the sources of meaning often as much as I can, especially creating communities and dialogues, experiences of the arts and seeking God. I have found making more meaning most gratifying. I feel sorrow for those people who do not try to do so. As Rev. William Sloane Coffin wrote, "It's a terrible thing that we settle for so much less." He called such people "boring" in *The Life of Meaning*, page 412.

44

TIME AND MEANING

Making more meaning and escaping from meaning (Sections 41-43) raise this fundamental question: what is the most meaningful (in the sense of "proper") way to spend our time and hence our lives?

Time is extremely important to meaning. It is the arena in which all meaning takes place. Without time there is no meaning except perhaps for God. Since making meaning emphasizes doing actions that have positive impacts, we need much time to do them, for examples, work and helping others. *We also require much time (years) to mature* so that we can both think and act well about our meaning (mostly in the sense of our "purpose").

As we all know well, *we rarely have as much time as we would like*, especially if we want to make meaning. Almost every task takes longer than the doer of it anticipates. *Such psychological (subjective) time is to us highly meaningful (in the sense of mentally "real").* Needless to say, *the shortage of time is quite frustrating, aggravating, and discouraging to us. It is also quite anguishing* because we fear generally that we will be unable to accomplish our tasks and reach our goals, or in other words, make the meaning that we want. Like nature, time has no respect for meaning.

The best metaphor that I can compare time to is a terrorist because it brutally instills fear in and attacks innocent people. Poets call time such derogatory terms as "devouring," "wasteful," "tyrannical," and "a predatory villain." We all are well aware that time leads to the decline and the biological death of all living things. Most sad, but true. *The terrorism of time is perhaps the hardest truth after death for humans to accept and deal with.*

Because of life's brevity, we ought to *strive to make as many moments as meaningful as we can. Every moment can be precious* because it is an opportunity to make meaning, for examples, having a great thought or feeling and falling in love with something or someone. We are given so little time, and it goes so fast, even the bad times! Try to make meaning as soon and quickly as you can without being too hasty.

We all much need to take the little time that we have very seriously as it measures the length of our lives in which we have to make meaning. *We all also need much to "make" time (= set aside some time to do a priority) to make meaning. What a person does with her time in effect determines what she feels and considers most meaningful (in the sense of "important") to herself.*

People everywhere fritter away even their free time. This is most mournful and dismaying to me. Why do they do this? After giving this question much thought, I decided that *the main reason that people "kill" their time is that they do not know how to make it more meaningful.* The consequence is that many people do not regard their time as highly meaningful. This is an excellent reason for everyone to constantly think about how they can make their lives have more meaning, especially by drawing more from its sources, so that they do not have to "kill" any of their time. (See Section 41 on escapes.)

We constantly battle between good (meaning) and evil (lack of positive meaning—see Section 52 on meaninglessness), with neither able to gain total superiority. *If a person uses her time to make meaning, she will ensure that good will prevail in her life.*

A reward of making time for meaning is that a person can focus on her big purposes in life. She will "make" time to do these. If there is an eternal afterlife, making time for meaning will surely merit it, not the "eternal fire" threatened by apostle Paul and the early church. Is this view of hell barbaric or is it fair to everyone who knows God's rules?

I myself try extremely hard to "make" as much time as I can. I am intent nearly to obsession—which one can be better?—with using every moment as meaningfully as I can. Although this view of time often frustrates me, what better way is there to live? As educator Jesse Stuart wrote, "Life is one's greatest possession. Life is one's all. And he should make every day, week, month, year count," quoted in Moorhead, editor, *The Meaning of Life,* pages 190-191. The only alternative to taking time to make meaning is to live as if one's time, and thereby life, matters little, even to oneself.

45

HOW WE MAY NOT BE FREE
TO MAKE MEANING

Throughout this work I have assumed that a person is free (= has an actual choice between two or more alternatives, not "free" in the political sense of having the right to do what one wants) to make meaning. *This assumption can be challenged by the very strong causal argument that (=) a person is physically but not directly caused or made to do what she does by many external factors.*

An extremely powerful type of cause (= anything that makes something else happen) is a person's conditioning (one's total environment that shapes a person's actions and beliefs, as psychologist B. F. Skinner was the first to emphasize).

A second extremely powerful type of cause of one's behavior is her inherited genes that gives the traits that she is born—actually conceived!—with. A person has to be who she is, intellectually and emotionally.

Thirdly, a person's subconscious, which some psychologists claim composes 90 per cent of a human's brain activity, can cause her to act irrationally from repressed factors such as fears and adverse childhood experiences.

There are many other types of causes, for examples, money and social class that may well determine one's entire life, as Marx held.

Conditioning, genes, and the subconscious—these highly powerful causes can make or force a person do, and even think, all that she does in the exact way that she does. Given all a person's causes, she can do only one action, according to the caused view. Of course, it is often quite hard to know "the cause" of an action because so many causes contribute.

A basic tenet in all the sciences, including the social or human ones, is that causes are strictly needed to explain any effect. How then can we be "free,"? *The "free-will question" is (=) "can a person freely choose, or is she forced by her causes to do only one action?" Doesn't a person always have reasons for what she does? If so, then*

don't these reasons literally make her do it? Don't causes or physical reasons force (make)
everything, including human actions, happen in the exact way that they do?

To give simple examples, if a person trips, she must fall and if it is very
hot and humid, we must sweat. Everything, including so-called "choices," must
have causes for them to happen precisely as they do. *On the other hand, free will*
explains nothing, not even why a person makes one choice rather than another.

THE MEANING OF BEING FREE OR CAUSED. Before I explain my
argument from meaning for some free will, I will briefly comment on the
meaning (in the sense of "importance") of being either free or caused. *No idea*
has more meaning (in the sense of "influence") than the free will question has in shaping
one's attitudes toward all people, including oneself.

Only if humans are free, are they responsible for the consequences of their
actions. So they should be praised or blamed for them. *We can be very judgmental*
about a free person.

On the other hand, if we are caused, we really cannot control the causes
on us. We are thereby not responsible for our actions, including our bad ones.
We should try to understand the harmful causes, especially on a criminal as well as all
other people. Then we need to provide them good (helpful) causes to counteract their (bad)
harmful ones. If a person's causes change, she herself changes, according to the
caused view of humans.

Finally, *if we have free will, we ought to regret our bad choices. We also ought to*
sometimes forgive ourselves and other people who have hurt us, if they sincerely apologize.
We should also apologize for our wrong choices.

Again on the other hand, the caused view holds that we should try to first
understand which factors cause our bad actions so that we can correct them
in the future without feeling regret about them. On this view, a person are not
burdened with agonizing over whether or not to forgive oneself and others who
have hurt them. They again need instead to understand the causes that made
these people hurt them.

In conclusion, free will would give humans much but inexplicable responsibility to
determine their actions to make meaning, whereas on the caused view humans would
make humans understandable, but not responsible for their actions. What question
other than whether we are free or caused has so much meaning (in the sense
of "importance") for how a person regards all humans, including herself?

46

AN ARGUMENT FROM
MEANING FOR FREE WILL

Now I shall present an argument from meaning that we are sometimes free. This argument much modifies one called "from deliberation" (= deep and careful thinking), which can be traced back to Aristotle, although he himself did not directly raise the free-will question. My modification from the point of view of meaning of his argument maintains that whenever you deliberate, a meaningful (in the sense of "new") idea can almost literally "pop" into your mind because such thinking is not mechanical. *If you think deeply and creatively enough, you can get a new, for you, idea that you were not caused to think in any way. Such an idea can be a genuine alternative (choice or option). However, this idea must also be meaningful (in the sense of "powerful") enough to overcome all your causes for you to make a free choice.*

An example of a free choice comes from a student studying for an exam. A student who studies to earn high grades to get a high-paying job or not to anger her parents is clearly caused to do so by her social conditioning. On the other hand, *if this student studies because she thinks hard, that is, deliberates, to get the new idea, for her, that studying solely to learn is meaningful (in the sense of "interesting for its own sake"), she chooses to study freely.* This idea has so much meaning (in the senses of "importance" and "power") to her that it can surmount all her previous causes so that she can make a free choice to study for the sake of learning material because it interests her.

Another example of a free choice: an alcoholic who deliberates the new meaningful idea, for her, that she is a person whose life has meaning rather than not makes a free choice. Alcoholics typically have to do this much to reform themselves.

Yet another example: the same holds for anyone who thinks deeply about how to make for herself a fulfilling but sustaining career, for example, writing novels with many implications about the meaning of life rather than working at a job that has to be done to make money to survive.

In each of these examples (interested student, reformed alcoholic, and fulfilled writer), a person has deliberated about what is meaningful for her to overcome all her past causes to be free to make a genuine choice from thinking of a new idea or option for herself.

Being free can be a lifestyle if a person deliberates often. Free choices can come from deliberating on a common sense level about one's life, although being educated and having a high intelligence often helps. Free acts are not that rare, although they certainly are not common. A free lifestyle arises whenever a person frequently deliberates to choose new actions instead of always acting from her causes. Deliberating is definitely hard to do, but it can become habitual. Every person needs to deliberate as much as she can about what her life can mean beyond her prior causes.

I myself have led a very free life since I have thought so intensely about the meaning of my life. I have deliberated many free choices for myself, for examples, to study and teach philosophy with an eye toward developing the idea of meaning, to attend numerous talks and artistic events and exhibits, and to read masterpieces of literature and good newspapers and magazines. I consider all these free choices because I deliberated to get them. I also consider all these choices worthwhile and far beyond my causes, especially conditioning.

Crucial to figuring out whether or not a person acts freely and thereby truly responsible to be praised or blamed for it depends *on how much mental effort she made for it or, in other words, how hard she tried to do it.*

47

THE LIFESTYLE OF A
MAKER OF MEANING

What lifestyle (way of living) follows from the eight sources of meaning? Almost needless to say, *it is one that is intelligently engaged in making more meaning in many areas.* The maker will attend many events of all types seeking more meaning in each. *She is a doer and difference-maker above all who tries to make as much positive difference as she can. A maker of meaning is dynamic and productive: activism is her hallmark.* For example, she would start out as probably one of the few active members in her community organization to improve the area for the people who live or work there. Then she rises to the highest level on which she can make the most meaning socially. (See Section 16 on making a social contribution.)

The lifestyle of a maker of meaning features much multi-tasking to make more meaning in the brief time that she has. I myself multi-task almost all my time except when I am reading, which requires single-minded concentration. Whenever I write, I multi-task by listening to the radio, cable TV, or the internet. If I am doing household or yard chores, I always wear headphones, usually listening to CDs and audio-cassette tapes—I am a technological dinosaur—to hear advanced ideas such as philosophy, cosmology, and the arts as well as listening to folk singer-songwriters. These musicians compose poetic lyrics for simple but beautiful melodies to make meaningful music (in the sense that it "combines highly rational and emotional elements"--see Sections 22 and 23 on these meanings in art.)

I admit that when I multi-task I do not do quite as well on both the chore and the listening, but I almost do: *I almost double my amount of meaning every day.* I consider multi-tasking a means to attain three meaningful (in the sense of "worthwhile") ends purposes or (goals) purposes or for me: (1) to write much about meaning and personal philosophy, (2) to keep growing as a person, especially intellectually by learning more, so that none of my days are limited to doing tedious chores, and (3) to do the most that I can those activities that I find most enjoyable.

The lifestyle of a maker of meaning is highly reflective as she tries to figure out the deep questions about "the meaning of it all." This may seem frustrating due to a lack of definite answers, but *it is very gratifying to know sounder and broader answers.* (See Section 70 on getting closer to truth.) A maker reads much, particularly books about the meaning of life, novels, and poetry implying the same topic— see Section 60--, issues that affect many people such as the environment—see Section 33--and the daily local newspaper, primarily for the area's arts and any events where she can find or make meaning.

A maker of meaning *tries to commit every day some time to creating community and social concerns.* (See Sections 15–17.)

A *meaning-maker loves artistic and cultural events*, especially films, lyrics in music, paintings with many interpretations, and serious but humorous plays. These arts in particular excel in creating meaningful ideas and emotions. (See Sections 22 and 23.) They also create highly enjoyable experiences, full of imagination and creativity which are our highest mental faculties. (See Section 21, #1 and #4).

Makers of meaning are essentially restless and wandering to find and make more meaning.

In summary, *in this lifestyle a person thinks and acts in many ways to make as much meaning as she can for others and herself.*

This lifestyle is fully enjoyable despite its amount of time required and its frustrations in dealing with others not motivated by meaning. Such a *lifestyle richly rewards a maker of meaning herself, but more importantly it benefits others. They ought to be the main concern of this lifestyle.*

Makers of meaning tend to be exceptional, but they can also be typical persons. (See Section 8 on who is a typical person.) Makers of meaning are driven internally. Does this drive reside in our genes in that a person is either born as a maker of meaning or not? There is not yet enough knowledge about human genes to answer this question. I myself suspect that genetic inheritance or a person's inborn personality produces most makers of meaning. However, I think that they can also be made to some extent by one's conditioning that determines which genes are actualized, especially when young.

I myself was much motivated by my neglected childhood to start my quest for meaning (see Section 9), but also by my genetic predispositions, for examples, caring and seeking, to live this lifestyle. I was also much motivated by my profound love of life. (See Section 9 again.)

What lifestyle could be better? At least it gives us a high ideal to strive toward. The current popular lifestyle consists of people pursuing mostly their own interests, often only materialism.

One of the most difficult and frustrating problems of making meaning is interesting people in it. Only a person can interest herself in anything: others can influence her only to a small extent usually. *Among my biggest sorrows has been how few interests people have in general. I am perplexed that so little can be done about that.*

This lifestyle is not as dramatic as that of existentialism which is the last (during the late 1960's and early 1970's) popular philosophy in the U. S. Existentialists such as Sartre and Camus tried to resist World War II heroically wresting meaning from what they called "our absurd world." Making meaning keeps alive this counter-cultural spirit, inspired by existentialism embodied in its short-lived hippie lifestyle and movement advocating peace, love, freedom and similar liberating values without this movement's naïve hopes and its drug and sexual excesses.

PART VI

MEANING OUGHT TO BE MOSTLY OBJECTIVE, NOT SUBJECTIVE

48

SUBJECTIVE AND
OBJECTIVE MEANING

A person can take two main views of meaning: subjective and objective. I have already mentioned these views several times in this book, but they are too complex to develop there. The subjective/objective distinction answers such key questions regarding meaning as the following ones with the stance of each view indicated after the colons:

(1) WHAT IS MEANING? Subjective: whatever an individual believes that it is. Objective: what something is in itself as much as we can know this.

(2) WHERE DOES MEANING RESIDE? Subjective: inside a person or in her mind. Objective: outside us or in external reality (the "world").

(3) HOW DO WE KNOW MEANING? Subjective: by believing that something has it. Objective: for facts, by appropriate observations up to the scientific method (rigorously testing hypotheses or informed guesses) and for opinions by logical, especially critical, reflection.

These differences are obviously major for making meaning, indeed.

The subjective view of meaning, or "subjective meaning" for short, of something consists of (=)"what a person believes is its significant impact on her." Subjective meaning is completely personal, but not private. "Subjective" refers only to what a person is conscious (aware) of. This is totally within or internal to each person. The subjective view may have uncorrectable errors in many cases because it has no external method of testing beliefs. A subjectivist is trapped in what philosopher R. B. Perry called "the egocentric predicament" in his *Present Philosophical Tendencies.*

For example, the subjective meaning of water to most people is that it "quenches thirst" because this trait usually impacts them the most. However, *the subjective meaning of water can vary much from person to person and to the same person at different times.* For example, to a person who falls into water, it means "wet," and to a chemist it signifies "two parts of hydrogen and one of oxygen." A person's experiences give her the subjective meaning of anything. This aspect of meaning largely results from a person's prejudices and biases which come from her personality and predispositions, for examples, being conservative or liberal and being a materialist or being an intangibilist.

I firmly believe that the current emphasis on subjective meaning has resulted in the biggest challenges to making meaning: meaninglessness, nihilism, and extreme relativism. The last of these challenges regards meaning as mostly subjective with disastrous results for our thinking and acting, as I will argue in Part VII.

The objective view of meaning, or "objective meaning" for short, much contrasts with the subjective. *The total objective meaning of anything consists of all its traits in itself external to (outside) or independent of anyone's perception of it. These traits compose the total truth (correspondence to reality) about anything.*

Objective meaning rests on a common sense view of the world as "out there." (See Section 8.) This view holds that big errors and distortions sometimes, but not often, can enter into complicated things when humans try to know them, for example, seeing a mirage of a puddle of water on the road ahead. If a person at first believes that the mirage is a puddle, she has a subjective meaning of it. Its objective meaning is that it is a mirage or a reflection of water on a hot day.

One's society establishes what is the objective meaning of anything to facilitate communication by deciding which traits of anything best define it by using Aristotle's rules for definition by genus and specific difference. (See Appendix I on definitions and Section 2 on defining "meaning.") If a definition of anything is found to be not objective, society can correct it by supplying its missing traits or by deleting its wrong ones in its dictionaries.

Objectivists in general hold that we can know the objective meaning of facts by means of the scientific method (experimental testing of a hypothesis or educated guess). (See Appendix I on induction.) They also maintain that we can partially know the objective meaning of even prescriptive values or intangibles by means of careful reasoning (thinking) with the laws of logic albeit with some indefiniteness. I call the combination of these scientific and logical methods "critical thinking." This enables us to know objective meaning as best that we can, although never completely except for simple things.

All thinkers today would agree that *the subjective and objective overlap much.* There is no sharp division between these two, for example, when a person knows by seeing skyscrapers repeatedly that they have the objective meaning of being very tall buildings with many floors. Skyscrapers can have the subjective meaning of being impressive with their power and might. For this example, the meaning is objective for most people, but it is both to most people, as are most things.

Since o*bjective meaning aims to give us truths, it is what we all ought to emphasize and live by. The subjective aspect is only sometimes important to a person,* usually for emotional reasons, for example, the ring given by a loving spouse at their wedding. A general example: a person who has a bad experience with something will be likely to give it a negative subjective meaning that will be quite important to her. My emphasis on objective meaning differs much from the current one of our society that meaning is mostly subjective. (See Section 55 on extreme relativism.)

I will next explore the reasons for thinking that meaning ought to be mostly subjective or mostly objective.

49

MEANING AS MOSTLY SUBJECTIVE

The view that can best answer the three main questions asked at the start of this Part is whether meaning ought to be conceived as either mostly subjective or mostly objective. This is a rather theoretical and difficult aspect of meaning, but it needs to be discussed because of its importance to answering these three key questions. The reader thereby may want to skip reading the rest of this Part, especially the arguments that meaning is objective because of their difficulty.

Almost all typical people and philosophers today firmly maintain that meaning is mostly subjective. The main reason that they give for this view is that people have many different views on the meaning of anything. Nobody has the authority to say which one is "right" or "correct." This position is strictly descriptive, not prescriptive. (See Section 4.)

Meaning is surely subjective to some extent, especially in knowing it and for personal emotional responses to it. A person needs to experience something in some way for it to have any meaning to her. The main question here is how subjective we ought to conceive meaning to be: somewhat or mostly. Surely not totally subjective because then literally "anything goes" for beliefs, for example, hateful Hitler thought that his murdering six million Jews had great positive (good) meaning because he detested them. Of course, almost everyone else thinks that this holocaust has meaning in the strictly negative (evil) sense that six million innocent humans were murdered. Something is seriously wrong with thinking that meaning is totally subjective.

The position that meaning is mostly subjective maintains that (=) the meaning of anything is whatever a person believes that it is except in two cases.

The first case of what is not strictly subjective on the mostly subjective position is obvious or simple facts, for example, the current time, date, and major historical events (if conventions regarding measuring these are accepted, as they should be). The second case that is not subjective according to this position is fundamental ethical principles, for examples, that and murdering and all other forms of hurting others physically and mentally, including lying as well as the basic principles telling us to do good actions innocent people is wrong. The typical subjectivist commonly calls these ethical principles, for examples, against murder and lies, "too different" to have varying subjective meanings dependent on an individual's beliefs. She would concede that the meaning of fundamental ethical principles are not mostly subjective, unlike all other beliefs except obvious physical facts just discussed.

However, another fundamental ethical principle according to the mostly subjective view is that whenever two of these principles conflict in a particular *case a person ought to do what she considers the highest or overriding one in this case. The reason for favoring the highest one can only be subjective,* since meaning is so variable and not objective on this view.

50

CRITICISMS THAT MEANING IS MOSTLY SUBJECTIVE

Should meaning be conceived of as mostly subjective? No, because this view tells us only what anything means to one person. This is the very small extent to which it is true. How valuable is this? Obviously little since a person can be horribly wrong, for example, racially prejudiced people. *The subjective view can tell us what a person thinks is the meaning of anything to her, but nothing else.* Surely this is trivial knowledge. Subjectivists have no way to prove even their beliefs to others since doing this is itself not subjective, but involves using the scientific method and other objective tests. Nor do they have a way of knowing the meaning of anything in itself, only to each person. A main question of this book is, "What is meaning really?" not what each person thinks that it is. (See Section 1 on the meaning-question. Please do not confuse "really" with, "absolutely" which is too strong here.)

That something is subjectively meaningful to someone surely does not make it so for anyone else, for example, serial murderer Jeffrey Dahmer who had a severe case of necrophilia (love of dead bodies) found eating and having sexual intercourse with males whom he murdered most meaningful. Thus, *dangerous chaos could result if this mostly subjective view is true.* Like Dahmer, any person could believe that the highest or overriding ethical principle of doing good by satisfying his need (for necrophilia) is the fundamental ethical one for him in some cases at least. This meaning cannot be proven to be wrong if meaning is mostly subjective. *This view of meaning isolates each person in her own beliefs and likes.*

Yet another major criticism of subjective meaning is that it results in mass mediocrity and complacency in which every person continues to believe whatever she has found meaningful. Why try to learn anything new if what you already know is meaningful enough to you? The same holds for actions. We ought to be active makers of meaning, not its passive observers, as if we were watching TV or a smartphone/computer screen.

I re-iterate that *the mostly subjective view is true only to the very limited extent that it tells us only what each person believes is the meaning of anything.* If meaning were mostly subjective, it would be trivial, chaotic, dangerous, and result in mass mediocrity. Meaning thus needs to be mostly objective.

51

MEANING OUGHT TO BE
MOSTLY OBJECTIVE

 $\mathbf{I}$ define the view that *meaning is mostly objective as (=) "the view that the meaning of anything ought to consist mostly of its main traits external to a person."* We *literally discover these traits* external to us by our senses for things and by thinking for ideas and values. That there is an actual world outside us is the basic assumption made by common sense. (See Section 8.) To deny this assumption is either academic or ridiculous. Yet, unlike the subjective view, it is quite difficult to completely conceive of anything in the objective view. It is even difficult to think that meaning can be objective! Accordingly, I will give four arguments that meaning is objective in Section 52.

I strongly maintain that *meaning ought to be thought of as mostly objective.* We ought to regard anything as existing external to us and in itself as much as we can.

The main reason that meaning ought to be mostly objective is that *we most need to know what things truly mean in themselves. This view gives us what is true or correct as opposed to possible self-delusions that the mostly subjective view can easily lead to, for example, blind faith in God.* (See Section 25 on blind faith.) *We need to use objective truths as the bases for our subjective meanings,* for examples, try to know the objective meaning of goodness and justice for social situations and problems. We much need to know objective meanings, not strictly subjective ones as hateful Hitler and Dahmer did.

I maintain that *even the meaning of intangibles, especially values, ought to be mostly objective* and that there are *objective truths—right and correct—about these. Such truths really do exist "out there" (outside our minds), but not in any physical place.* We ought to try to know these as best that we can by thinking in accord with the laws of logic. (See Appendix I.) I believe that our difficulty in knowing the objective meaning of intangibles is the main reason that we have so much uncertainty and ignorance about life's biggest questions and values.

So, I contend that we ought to think that the meaning of both facts and values as mostly objective because this view gives us truths in themselves insofar as we can know them. The subjective view expresses a strong emotional element which can know little about truths. Meaning ought to be mostly subjective only when emotions are most relevant. This is rather rare.

As we look around the world today, we see troubles everywhere, for examples, poverty, selfishness, corporate greed, terrorism, genocide, constant wars and many others. *At times these troubles seem hopeless. Yet, we also see thinkers and philosophers, especially postmodernists (the view that there is no one truth for anything) and extreme relativists, not helping to soothe any of these, but insisting instead that they are mostly subjective and thereby not able to be known true for anyone except each person. (I owe these ideas to an eloquent letter written in 1995 by my longtime auto-didactic friend, Rev. C. Lee Hubbell.) Solutions to the troubles cited above surely have many disputed or gray areas, but they also have objective ideas that can rectify them. I contend that we can finally begin to take a stance on solving these troubles by thinking in terms of objective meaning.*

52

ARGUMENTS THAT
MEANING IS OBJECTIVE

It is important to be sure that meaning is truly objective, especially intangibles. Remember that the logically-weak view that meaning is mostly subjective is extremely popular today. Hence, I will give four arguments for its objective reality. Like the arguments for intangibles, these four arguments are quite abstract, difficult to comprehend and theoretical, but are essential to counteract today's mostly-subjective view with its horrific results. The reader may want to skip—yet still again!—reading them.

1. THE WORLD EXISTS INDEPENDENTLY OF US. *The main argument for the objectivity of meaning is that things obviously exist on their own, external or independent of us with their own meaning in themselves.* This objective view that the world exists external to us rests on the most fundamental tenet of common sense. For example, the belief that a car really exists external to humans is just plain common sense to the typical person, but not to many philosophers today!

We all must be quite careful that what we believe is the objective meaning of something is really the truth (corresponds to external reality). For a thing, knowing truths is a simple matter of determining what are the facts about it by using the simplified scientific method. For example, a person needs to know the facts about a table to know its meaning, but these are rather easy to obtain. Facts in themselves are obviously objective, even though we are occasionally mistaken about them. This is not a reason to give up common sense, as major philosophers such as Georg Hegel and F. H. Bradley and today's dominant analytic and anti-realist ones today do and devote themselves mostly to parsing sentences and to minutely analyzing how we can say or know anything.

Intangibles as such exist as totally abstract truths. *We literally discover them* by deep thinking about them: we do not merely make them up or abstract them from our sensations of things because they are not even implicit there.

For example, justice cannot be found in just situations by our senses, but by thinking deeply about it. Justice is such a complex intangible that few people can know many of its component truths. Nevertheless, these truths exist outside us metaphorically "awaiting" our minds to find them one at a time.

Plato similarly maintained that what he called "Ideas" exist external to us in their own "immaterial world," not just in our minds which come to know them. (See Section 35 and 63 on Plato.) He maintained that Ideas exist on a level transcending material things. Many of his arguments that these Ideas exist as objective intangibles are so complicated that they cannot be summarized here. One of his more graphic arguments for his view on this is that the physical world "weakly reflects" perfect and eternal truths. He famously compared these two worlds to a prisoner in a cave who escapes to the far bigger world of Ideas that exists outside it. (See Diagram 2 on Plato's allegory of the cave in Section 33.) The Platonic way of knowing these Ideas is by discovering their objective proportions of geometrical forms such as circles, squares, and triangles. (See Section 24 on Plato's conception of beauty and argument 3 in Section 36.)

The objectivity of these forms is grounded by the next argument. Philosophers Bertrand Russell and Alfred North Whitehead in their three-volume *Principia Mathematica* (1913) rigorously proved that all mathematics and hence geometry rigorously derives from logic.

2. THE LAWS OF LOGIC ARE OBJECTIVE. All *thinking about meaning (and everything else) ought to conform to the laws of logic. These laws are objective because they exist external to us as patterns of relationships in our ideas and thinking;* for examples, be consistent or do not contradict yourself, use the scientific method to determine facts, and always think in arguments. (See Appendix I on logic in general for more objective laws of logic.) *These objective logical patterns and laws of logic apply to all thinking in all societies at all times.* If the laws of logic were subjective, societies would devise different ones. These logics would not make sense in other societies—and even their own! *Only if the laws of logic are objective in applying to the world can they helpfully guide our thinking which is highly subjective.*

Following these laws is far preferable to relying on the highly varying psychology of individual thinking as subjective meaning does. *Particularly logic's laws of induction and the scientific method must be objective because they have applied so successfully to the physical world in many complex and amazing technologies,* for examples, computers (the most amazing one to me), cars, TV, and many other developments in engineering. Only if the laws of logic are objective could all these fabulous technologies reflect and apply to the physical world so well.

Some current philosophies such as phenomenology use the word "logic" for a way of thinking that is artistic and so highly subjective. For example, philosopher Martin Heidegger maintained in one of his essays that a painting of a pair of peasant's shoes "spoke" to him—he did not specify what they said! Such a logic is quite subjective and hence not universal, but artistic thinking is a special usage of "logic," not its main one or its definition. (See Section 2 and Appendix I on definitions of words.)

3. NATURAL LAWS ARE OBJECTIVE. *A closely related argument for the objectivity of meaning comes from natural laws (= rules that govern and derive from the world). These laws are externally embedded in nature,* for examples, the laws for the survival, nutrition, and reproduction of all animal species. Like intangibles such as consciousness, these laws exist objectively in the physical world just as much as colors, temperatures, shapes, and sizes do, although not in a physical way. Natural laws reside "out there" in the world outside our minds. We need to try to know them as they exist objectively in nature, not subjectively or only in our minds which may well be believed but wrong for centuries, as many scientific theories were, for example, Aristotle's physics fundamentally assumes that everything, even inanimate (lifeless) things, move toward goals.

4. VALUING VERSUS EVALUATING. *A person can subjectively value or personally "prize," as Dewey often put it, anything for no given reason. Valuing can be totally subjective. An evaluation, on the other hand, consists of giving objective reasons for a judgment.* For example, beholding a sunset can be valued by a person who just enjoys it and does not give any reasons for valuing it. To evaluate a sunset, on the other hand, a person needs to give objective reasons, for examples, a sunset's magnificent colors, its stark forms, and the contrasting drama of their movement. Then an evaluator can make a conscious judgment about the worth of a sunset based on these reasons. These evaluative reasons are objective because they belong to the sunset itself, not just an observer's subjectively valuing it. The objective reasons are often quite hard to know and to describe in words, like those needed for evaluating a sunset.

As is probably obvious by now, for a very long time *I myself feel revulsed if meaning is mostly subjective or up to each person to determine.* (See Section 56 on my criticisms of extreme relativism.) What if a person believes, for a general example, that an evil is meaningful? Like extreme relativism, the subjective aspect of meaning can tell us only what each person believes about anything. This very often is little more than trivial information, but it is simple and easy. No wonder that the idea of meaning has been undeveloped and neglected since the shallow and oversimple subjective view of it has ascended since the start of the modern era in the middle of the seventeenth century. (See Section 2 on the etymology of "meaning" and Section 65 on the meaning of life in the modern period.)

PART VII

CHALLENGES TO MEANING

53

MEANINGLESSNESS AND HOW TO LESSEN IT

Next I will treat the main challenges to meaning (mostly in the sense of "significance"). I think that the following are the major opponents to it with an indication why each threatens meaning in a frontal way: (1) meaninglessness, which maintains that something severely lacks meaning, (2) nihilism, which holds that nothing has meaning in the end, and (3) extreme relativism, which argues that the meaning of anything is whatever a person believes that it is.

(1) Meaninglessness has never been so prevalent as in recent years. Many factors have caused this, for examples, the loss of traditional values, our continually declining economy, being depersonalized by smartphones, fragmented families, and many other factors. "Meaninglessness" is quite hard to define, but very easy to feel. *This word refers mostly to either (1) a lack of positive meaning or (2) negative or no meaning.* I will treat only the lack of positive meaning because negative meaning refers to its nonexistence about which we can say nothing. An obvious example of this second sense of "meaninglessness" is death. Every person needs much meaning in their life to accept this gracefully in themselves and their loved ones.

By the logical law of consistency of word usage, "meaninglessness" ought to refer to "lacking meaning," but today it almost always denotes "having no meaning (in the sense of "relevance").

A very troublesome use of "meaningless" is to refer to something that has a "bad" meaning. This usage often sounds strange, but it is correct nonetheless to say, for example, that "pain is meaningless," in the sense that it lacks good meaning, not that it has no meaning. Remember that "meaning" usually denotes good or positive meaning. (See Section 2 on "meaning.")

Meaninglessness in one's life can be very sorrowful, crippling, and even devastating. Imagine the the sadness that a person feels the first time that she realizes that her life lacks meaning (in the sense of "significance")! *Most meaninglessness is internal or within us.* A person may feel that her life is worthless, pointless, futile, and trivial. Human woes are well expressed in *Ecclesiastes* (especially verse 12, chapters 1–8), an early book of the Bible. This book summarizes all our woes when it famously exclaims, "'Meaningless! Meaningless!,' says the teacher, 'All is meaningless!'" (Notice that *The New International Version of the Bible* in 1984 translates the traditional Hebrew word for "vanity" as "meaningless.")

Today many people are forced to work long and hard at mostly meaningless jobs just to financially support themselves and their families. Worse, our minds can easily raise doubts about even our most cherished beliefs. Worst, we tend to dwell on negative aspects of our lives such as frustrations, discouragements, disappointments, regrets, and many other feelings of meaninglessness. So we have many sources of it. Our lives have a large dark side, as existentialists Dostoevsky, Kierkegaard, Camus, and Sartre were the first to emphasize.

I stressed at the start of this book that if a person lacks meaning too much for her, she will commit suicide. (See Section 7.) I also stressed that lacking meaning such as a poor childhood relationship with one's parents can cause a person to commit violence because a major lack of meaning can make her uncontrollably angry. (See Section 7 again.) People become angrier and act increasingly irrational the more meaningless that they feel, as prominent senses of the word "meaningful" are "rational" and "makes sense."

LESSENING MEANINGLESSNESS: We all need to address the meaninglessness in our lives so that we can lessen it. To be sure, this is a hard task, but *it helps much to study meaning.* In general, the more you know about meaning, the less meaninglessness that you will feel. Then a person can eventually use this knowledge to change her beliefs or to perform actions that can make her life a little more meaningful. Many of these changes will involve implementing more of the sources of meaning, for examples, making quality relationships and finding fulfilling work. A person needs free will or inventiveness to think how to apply these sources to herself and then she needs a strong will (desire) to carry them into practice. (See Sections 45 and 46.)

Another way to lessen meaninglessness in one's life is to concentrate on meaningfulness. (Remember that this cumbersome term refers to positive or good meaning just as the word "meaning" often does. See Section 2.) Some of the other sources of meaning that can best counteract meaninglessness are a sense of community, dialogue, and buying possessions—but briefly! (See Section 34 criticizing materialism.)

Life! Life! Life! *Let us live our brief and fast lives as meaningfully as we can by plunging deeply into all the sources of meaning* instead of shallowly escaping in fear of them. Let meaning inspire us to do the most that we can with our lives. Finally, let us study meaning directly and explicitly most of all.

We can in these ways much lessen but never eliminate all meaninglessness from our lives: the ultimate meaninglessness of biological death confronts all living beings.

54

TOTAL MEANINGLESSNESS: NIHILISM

Nihilism arose as a movement after the utterly horrific destruction of the two World Wars in the twentieth century. I define "nihilism" as (=) the view that "nothing really matters in the end, that our lives have no positive meaning (in the senses of 'value' and 'purpose')." This extreme view goes further than saying that we have meaninglessness in our lives: it says that our lives are totally meaningless eventually. As despairing Macbeth famously exclaimed, "our lives are full of sound and fury, signifying nothing" (act 5, scene 4). Thus, *nihilism poses the biggest challenge to the view that our lives have meaning. To be entitled by logic to believe that your life does have meaning, you must first refute nihilism.* This is neither easy nor simple to do!

Nihilists basically believe that nothing that a person does matters to the universe and that everything that we do will result in nothing. The word "nihilism" derives from Latin for nothing. Even heroic acts will not matter from the point of view of time and the universe. Much that we do is for perpetuating ourselves, but why do this? To raise children to do the same? Doing this has no point if our lives do not have one. Professor Garrett Thompson remarked that to halt such an infinite regress (repeating endlessly) we need "a purpose that is guaranteed to be meaningful in and of itself" (*On the Meaning of Life, page 48*). Of course, nihilists do not think that such a purpose can be found.

According to nihilism, all our pursuits are ultimately senseless and empty. Camus compared our lives to the futile chore of Sisyphus (who eternally pushes a big rock up a steep hill only to have it keep falling down because he denied that the Greek gods exist, according to the myth about him). Camus, who was not a nihilist himself, called the human condition "absurd" (makes no sense). To him, we live in an alien (foreign) and unresponsive world.

The philosopher who advocated nihilism the strongest was Arthur Schopenhauer. His main argument for nihilism is that we get what we desire so rarely that we are bound to be unhappy. Professor Mihaly Csikszentmihaly, who popularized the idea of flow (making optimal or best experiences), wrote that, "life is, by itself, meaningless" in *Flow, page 215.*

Singer-songwriter Bob Dylan sang that we have "no direction home." I interpret this metaphor as he has no way to know how to get to his true self. (Only meaning can!) We cannot live authentically in our overpopulated world made worse by our bad actions and foolish inactions. Death definitely ends our making meaning at least on earth which is all that we can know for sure. Tolstoy wrote in his novella (short novel) *The Death of Ivan Ilyich* that, "death is the truth." In these ways nihilism poses the most vexing challenge to making meaning: why bother making meaning?

55

REFUTING NIHILISM: MEANING'S PROPER PERSPECTIVE IS OUR LIVES

If we cannot refute nihilism, there may well be no meaning in our lives after all. Perhaps it is the universe's big joke on all of us! Ha! Ha!

Nihilism is an extremely pessimistic and negative view of life, to be sure. How can we refute it, as all of us must do to logically believe in meaning? My own answer is the following: *all nihilists emphasize that our lives are meaningless (in the sense of "insignificant") from the perspective of the universe and all time. Yet, this perspective is surely much too big. The proper perspective for meaning is a person's life.*

Surely we can do meaningful acts (in the sense of "good") for ourselves and others. We all can leave legacies by living meaningful lives that inspire others. (See Section 70 on legacies.) Surely such actions give our lives meaning (in the sense of "purpose"). *Meaningful actions certainly make a difference, at least for a time.* How is this absurd? The earth may well be, but humans are not because *we have a thinking ability that transcends (goes beyond) it and enables us to think of purposes, know intangible truths, and make free choices.* Our lives certainly do have moments of meaning. Not only does the *meaning that we make have effects, but also it can mushroom in people whom we influence even remotely.* (See Sections 16 and 17 on the umbrella effect.) We thus for a time can make our lives and those of others more meaningful, not nothing as nihilists insist. *Meaningfulness is a fantastic and joyous state.* We do not have to matter to the entire universe and all time to have meaning.

To summarize these criticisms of nihilism: the universe and eternity are much too big perspectives for meaning; human lives are the proper one. I think that all these reasons are enough to refute nihilism and to be entitled by logic to start making meaning.

I myself was a nihilist during the skeptical rages of my youth because I could find nothing worthwhile, including myself. (See Section 1.) I overcame this by seeking and making meaning and dwelling in its many mansions.

56

EXTREME RELATIVISM: MEANING DEPENDS ON A PERSON'S BELIEFS

Closely connected to nihilism but not pessimistic, *"extreme relativism"* *defined as (=) the view that "meaning depends on (is relative to) the beliefs of each person."* *According to this view, the meaning of anything is what a person believes that it is. This* *view is very widely prevalent today.* It is currently the view that both the typical person and the professor of philosophy endorse: starting in the modern era, "After Descartes we have come to see ourselves as almost infinitely free assigners of meaning who can give whatever meaning we choose to the meaningless objects around us," wrote professors Dreyfuss and Kelly in *All Things Shining:* *Reading the Western Classics to Find Meaning in a Secular World, page 139.* Like nihilism, *extreme relativism poses another big challenge to making meaning* because if all beliefs are relative, even acts such as racist and sexist ones are meaningful if someone believes that they are. This view assumes that meaning is totally subjective. *Extreme relativism conceives and assumes that all reality exists on the* *descriptive level, nothing is prescriptive. (See Section 4.)*

Extreme relativists emphasize the wide diversity of beliefs on many topics. They insist that there is no absolute standard that holds for everyone with no exceptions. Even Pope Francis has recently asked, "Who am I to say what is right or wrong?" about homosexual marriages. "If it feels good, do it," "different strokes for different folks," and "to each his own" are some of today's many popular sayings that imply extreme relativism.

Each person is entitled to decide what anything means to her, according to this philosophy. Everyone reigns sovereign over what she considers the meaning of anything. "Who's to say what anything means?" an extreme relativist asks with the obvious answer, "No one but each person." At least you are entitled to your own opinions! Extreme relativists tolerate these as just "differences." This philosophy reflects the current widespread postmodernism (the rejection of modern philosophy's position that there are objective or external truths). The typical person similarly holds hard an extreme relativism that she uses as her trump card in any disagreement by saying, "It's all relative. You are entitled to your opinion." Extreme relativism thereby confuses the political (a person's right to believe) with the ethical (what is right). This is the first of many criticisms of extreme relativism.

57

CRITICISMS OF EXTREME RELATIVISM

Extreme relativism implies the view that meaning is mostly subjective. As such, it shares its severe criticisms of being chaotic, trivial knowledge, potentially dangerous and results in mass mediocrity. (See Section 48 on criticisms of meaning as mostly subjective.)

This version of relativism extends this view even further and allows a person to believe whatever she thinks is meaningful, including even simple facts such as that the earth is flat, as the members of the International Flat Earth Society believe today! *Doesn't extreme relativism allow many other self-centered and biased beliefs which can easily be twisted to favor whatever a person feels inclined to believe?*

The meaning of anything surely depends on more than what a person believes that it is. Some of a relativist's beliefs, particularly complex ones, surely can be false or wrong. More important by far is knowing the objective meaning of anything in itself, as I have emphasized. (See especially Sections 51 and 52.)

If meanings were so relative, *we would not have a shared standard to judge anything and anybody*, since this would depend on whatever each person believes that it is. *Many people would probably not be able to identify any judging standards for themselves.* This is no small matter for philosophy which is most distinctive because it prescribes standards and values, not describes things and facts as the sciences do. (See Section 4.)

Extreme relativists are extremely tolerant because they hold that nothing can be proven objectively true, but it is easy to be too tolerant of others' beliefs, for example, should you tolerate someone who believes that it is meaningful to murder you? Such relativists can answer from the point of view of the logical law of consistency only that what is meaningful to you just "differs" from what it is to a murderer, racist or sexist. (See Section 48.) *They cannot compare with logical*

147

warrant themselves as better than primitive savages except to say that they are "different" from us. So must logically be a murderer, to them.

A final criticism: *who should win if an extreme relativist disagrees with her society* about an ethical issue such as abortion or capital punishment? Society invariably will win and prevail simply since it is bigger and more powerful. Yet, many societies are corrupt and often oblivious to justice and ethics unless they are forced to be so.

Even though these criticisms are severe, they still allow that *extreme relativism is true, but to a lesser degree by far: everything ought to be relative (related) to its circumstances or context to help determine its objective meaning.* In other words, a person needs to relate everything to its situation or context in order to help find out what it objectively or truly means. Again, the meaning (and truth) about anything does not depend on what a person believes that it is, but on what it objectively (actually) is.

I emphasize that the truth of relativism is quite minor, especially in view of that of the absolutes of meaning, which I will briefly explain next. I hope that these criticisms dispose of *extreme relativism as overly subjective and simplistic in general.*

As may be obvious by now, I myself have strongly opposed extreme relativism for many years. I have seen the *devastating effects on individuals and society of thinking that practically anything is as meaningful as anything else, for examples, poor career choices, weak stances on ideas, feeble judgments about values, refusals to condemn obvious wrongs and shallow social standards such as materialism*—to name a few. Extreme relativism can be quite damaging to both our thinking and acting. Today's leaders, except religious fanatics, offer few positive guidelines, a crying need now. *Many academic disciplines stand for little today. What idea is better to stand for than making meaning? This is particularly true for philosophy. No one seems to know how to tell right or wrong and true or false except for themselves. Many typical people thereby have little to live for besides their nuclear families, materialism, and blind faith in God.*

Meaning has met its major challenges in Part VII of meaninglessness (can be much lessened, but not eliminated), nihilism (takes the too big perspectives of infinity and eternity, not the proper one of a person's life) and especially extreme relativism (many major criticisms but true in a limited sense).

I firmly maintain that *the last of these challenges is the biggest problem now facing our thinking and acting. Doing both of these in terms of the absolutes of meaning (which I will explain next) andthe mostly objective meaning of each case is my proposed solution.* (See Conclusions in Section 58.)

58

THREE ABSOLUTE
ABSOLUTES OF MEANING

*A*ny *person or society who lives without an absolute drifts in uncertainty without an anchor.* This is a very sad situation, indeed. We much need solid and shareable absolutes to guide us through it to lead the most meaningful (in the sense of "best") lives that we can. An absolute is (=) a universal principle that applies to everyone. (See Section 1 on meaning as an absolute.)

An absolute in its descriptive sense applies without any exceptions." There are *absolute facts,* for examples, the speed of light (186,000 miles per second—extremely fast!), absolute cold (-459° Fahrenheit, at which all atomic motion stops—brrr!) and perhaps absolute hot (at the Big Bang). (See Section 27 on the Big Bang.)

However, *the main sense of "absolute" is not factual: it is prescriptive* which tell us what we all ought to do in general. (See Section 4.) Such absolutes can give us standards and guidelines to live by and judge everything which we certainly much need now, as I have emphasized.

We also need more than negative absolutes such as "do not murder" and "do not discriminate unfairly" because these tell us only what we ought not to do. Fortunately, there are many positive absolutes that tell us what we ought to do, for examples, give people the respect that they deserve, maximize free choices compatible with those of others, and maintain the balance of all parts of the environment. Unfortunately, these absolutes often conflict when applied to concrete cases, for example, should you get help for a drug-addicted friend whom you promised not to tell about? This question involves a conflict of the absolutes of promise-keeping and helpfulness. Such conflicts seem to make exceptions to every absolute so that they do not seem absolute. However, I think that second-order *absolutes of meaning or what I call "absolute absolutes" have no exceptions,* even in conflict with other absolutes as first-order absolutes do as I shall show next.

A first *example of an absolute absolute: whenever a person makes a judgment, she ought to always consider the objective meaning of all its major factors as much as she can. Prominent examples of these factors include its physical effects, the people affected, the money involved, and other factors that vary in each case.* It is certainly not easy to know all these, but every person ought to make an honest effort to do so.

Everyone everywhere ought to follow this first absolute absolute to ensure that we consider the objective meaning of anything as fully as we can. Doing this will not solve a problem, but it will certainly clarify its issues much by bringing our attention to its main factors.

A *second absolute absolute more directly addresses meaning: show care (concern in compassionate and kind ways) as much as you can about the positive meaning (meaningfulness) of anything.* I call this the "absolute of caring." We all ought to direct our wills in a concerned way toward affirmative meaning. Psychologists can explain little about caring. This aspect of the will may well be an extra- or super-rational part of humans, like intuitions. (See Section 39.) Socrates implored his "children" (disciples) to care only about living the good life. (See Section 61 and recall that meaning includes all the greatest values, including the good. See Section 3.)

If we just care about the meaning of a problem, we will go a long way toward solving it because our other major faculties like thinking and feeling will follow along. This way will not guarantee that we all will do good acts or know truths, but it is the most that we can do in our extremely complex world with our limited faculties for knowing. If we are caring, we will also be curious and motivated. These excellent traits will help a person make more meaning.

Caring about positive meanings includes being attentive to negative ones to lessen them as much as you can, of course.

A *third—and hardest—absolute absolute of meaning is that every person ought to make as much meaning as she can.* Why wouldn't a person prefer all the meaning that she can get? Common sense tells us that it is better to have more meaning, broader purposes and bigger truths rather than the timid and small ones offered by the current corrosive extreme relativism and postmodernism which results in shallow thinking and even danger around the world today (see Section 57), for example, ISIS believes that it is most meaningful to terrorize people who do not share their fanatical view of Islam. This third absolute absolute of meaning would be quite difficult for most of us to follow freely—see Sections 45 and 46 on free choice—in our shallow society. (See Section 43 on making more meaning.)

59

THE ULTIMATE ABSOLUTE ABSOLUTE: MAXIMIZE MEANING

We can *combine these three absolute absolutes--(1) consider the objective meaning of factors; (2) care about the positive ones; and (3) make as much meaning (meaningfulness) as you can--into one ultimate absolute absolute:* "maximize meaning *(meaningfulness)* as much as you can in every situation by considering its major factors and caring for the positive ones."

For short, I call this combination of absolute absolutes "maximize meaning." (The last word is a short form for the awkward-sounding "meaningfulness"—see Section 2.) I believe that this is the ultimate absolute absolute or best basic standard because it combines three major absolute absolutes.

What a person needs to strive to do regarding every question and for every problem is to try to maximize meaning as much as she can. To do this, we need to determine what is most meaningful according to the definition of "meaning" as "the significant impact of anything" and its other senses. (See Sections 2 and 3.)

Maximizing meaning often can again (see Section 39 on testing intangible truths) be known only indefinitely; for example, future events which usually are little more than informed guesses. (So are many decisions in our lives, for example, career and marital choices!)

This ultimate absolute absolute applies differently relative to each case in its main factors such as effects, people, costs, and varying considerations. These variations incorporate the limited truth of relativism that "the meaning of anything ought to be applied to its situation." (See the end of Section 58.)

We all (everyone everywhere always) ought to follow the three absolute absolutes of meaning in the ultimate one. These can best guide and direct our lives.

CONCLUSION: THE METHOD OF MAKING MEANING: EXAMPLE OF PERSONAL ETHICS. Today's rootless society and most individuals in it desperately need absolute absolutes such as maximizing meaning. In the present time we much need something more to believe in and live by besides the age's stressful materialism (both monetary and metaphysical) and blind faith in God. Absolute absolutes can restore fundamental prescriptive values such as goodness, beauty, justice, and truth that we know so little about today. These values could have tremendous meaning for us. The fully developed idea of meaning can give us access to these values on its firm foundation at last, but this would be too long and too much theory for this book. (See Section 8 on common sense.)

Nevertheless, this idea of meaning can also finally give us highly worthwhile ideas and values that we can firmly believe and stand for in these days of narrow knowledge with unlimited data in our hand-held smartphones. This idea is a great desideratum (required need) today.

The absolute absolutes can be formulated as a method of making meaning.

The method of making meaning *first insists that we all ought to emphasize knowing and acting on as much as we can the objective meaning of anything under consideration* such as all problems, situations, interests, things, ideas and so on, as maximizing meaning urges us all to do. *We all ought to ask first what is the mostly objective meaning of each case. In the end we ought to act on whatever outcome would be most meaningful (usually in the sense of "fulfilling") to all involved.*

Perhaps the best example of what crying need that making meaning can satisfy is ethics because it specifies what is good. This field is central to good human relationships and actions, our well-being and happiness. Yet, thanks mostly to extreme relativism and postmodernism, ethics has now come to be widely construed as only what each person thinks that it is without any basis for agreement. No one today knows how we can agree on a standard for determining right or wrong. We regard all current ethical theories (which identify the greatest good, for examples, emphasizing results [utilitarianism], doing duties [duty ethics] and being practical [pragmatism]) as just "different" theories on what is morally good to do, not as ideas that can settle a moral problem. *So, ethics today is no help in solving our many moral problems.* (See Sections 56 and 57 on extreme relativism and its criticisms.)

I suggest that we can satisfy our current crying need for a guiding ethics by the method of making meaning. For any ethical problem, we ought first to determine the objective meaning of a moral problem as best (most) that we can. This requires thorough investigation and then careful thinking, especially trying to eliminate all personal biases and to emphasize the objectively meaningful (in the sense of "the most significant impacts") factors present. At this stage we ought to follow the first absolute absolute of considering all the major moral factors involved. Then we ought to employ the second absolute absolute to show much care (concern) to determine which factor is the most meaningful (in the sense of "leading in the most positive or life-affirmative action in general").

There is no way to measure this except enlightened common sense. Finally, a person ought to act on this factor as the most ethical one. In other words, she ought to make the most positive meaning (meaningfulness) that she can while she realizes that she cannot eliminate all meaninglessness in a moral problem.

PERSONAL ETHICS. I can very briefly indicate here how the method of meaning can give birth to the needed field of personal ethics. *A big part of personal ethics consists of taking the first step of recognizing the meaning (in the sense of "significance") of the ethical good.* To do this is to strongly recognize that some situation or action raises questions about moral value or worth that strikes you strongly because of their fundamental worth to you as a person. I call this "the ethical dimension" of human life. We all ought to directly confront this dimension whenever it arises in our daily lives and emphasize that we are faced with determining what is good to do, not just what is practical. Then we will be fully motivated to fully examine all the major factors in each case.

The next stage of personal ethics consists of finding the most meaningful (in the sense of "significant impact") ethical standard for making moral decisions. For this we all ought to try to get higher and higher standards. Declining, low or weak moral standards were a major reason for the fall of Rome--and the U. S.--and of all the tragic characters in Shakespeare: Hamlet, Macbeth, Lear, Othello, Julius Caesar, and some of the kings of England. *The same fatal fall can happen to any individual who has declining or low ethical standards.* Materialistic standards are often the lowest even though they can improve us physically, whereas high standards derived from our duties (debts) or obligations to others improve us.

A code of high ethical standards can lead to a morality enlightened more than the social one, for examples (with the high standard indicated in parentheses), Socrates (never stop seeking the true and the good), Jesus (love even your enemies), H. D. Thoreau (be self-reliant) and Abraham Lincoln, Gandhi, King, and Nelson Mandela (unite opposing groups nonviolently). At least an enlightened code of high moral standards will lead to a more meaningful personal ethics that can solve the myriad of moral problems that everyone faces, for examples, lying and cheating if not caught, (See Appendix II for examples of personal and social ethical problems.)

I still have much work to do developing a personal ethics, but it can serve as an example of the start of method of making meaning.

Can't we agree that the method of making meaning is, what we all ought to live by? I myself certainly cannot think of any idea more fundamental, helpful, broader, universal—see Section 1—or better overall.

PART VIII

THE MEANING OF LIFE

60

A DEFINITION OF "THE
MEANING OF LIFE"

In Arthur Miller's tragic drama *Death of a Salesman (1949)* the protagonist Willy Loman takes his own life because he does not consider himself successful in finding the meaning of life in materialism and popularity. This acclaimed play frontally although implicitly raises the question of what is the meaning of life for the typical person in our times.

I come next to the idea of the meaning of life as distinct from the idea of meaning which I have been developing hitherto in all the previous Sections. *The meaning-of-life question asks (=), "What is the purpose or point of my life?" This is the broadest and best question that a person can ask about herself. The meaning of life is crucial to one's self-concept, happiness, and much more. It is what your life really ought—notice its primary prescriptive sense (see Section 2)—to be all about according to you.* Your view on the meaning of life determines how you ought to live your life according to several of it sources. The meaning of your life in its descriptive sense records how you actually live it.

I believe that *there is one meaning of life for all people, but this takes a different form for each person.* We all share the sources of meaning to varying degrees because we are quite similar as humans biologically and in our basic needs. This is my response to Professor Owen Flanagan's assertion that, "The worst question to ask is, 'What is the meaning of life?' There is no single meaning of life" (*The Really Hard Problem, page 201*).

So what is the meaning of life? Every word of this question is problematic, asserts Professor Terry Eagleton, *The Meaning of Life, page 78.* The meaning-of-life question sounds grand and "implies a profundity and seriousness," according to Professor John Cottingham in his *On the Meaning of Life, page 21.* Indeed, the phrase "the meaning of life" does sound this way, but I do not think it is so grand and profound because it applies to the daily life of the typical person. (See the summary of Baggini's book in Section 69.) *This humble meaning should consist of several sources at least.* I will next briefly describe what I consider its main ones.

A. HIGH QUALITY RELATIONSHIPS ARE THE MAIN MEANING OF LIFE

The main source of the meaning of life is high quality relationships with other people because humans are so social in nature. We are the most social animal. For this reason, much of the meaning of life is to have loving and helpful relationships with as many people as you can without overextending yourself, as Kant in his *Critique of Practical Reason* advised us in what he called "the categorical imperative," known in simpler terms as the "Golden Rule" which is found in all the world religions.

Try to have the biggest purpose that you can with all the people you relate to. You yourself are not the full meaning of your own life. This meaning is closely connected to other people.

As Terkel quipped to David Friend and the editors of *Life* magazine, *The Meaning of Life*, the meaning of life is "to *make a dent!*" Presumably, making a dent mostly involves having a positive difference on others such as improvements, inventions, and inspiration as well as material help. Terkel added—at 91!--that when you do this, "*you feel like you count*" quoted in *The Life of Meaning, page 110.* He made it clear in his other books that *this feeling can come only from altruism (caring mostly for others) rather than egoism (caring mostly for oneself—see Appendix II on ethics) in one's motives. The same holds true for all making meaning.*

Helping others is not easy to do. It involves giving time, energy, compassion, money, and more. Plus, we must be sure that we do not violate others' dignity and pride when we help them. That is often the reason that the other resists or refuses another's help.

Some examples of helping other people include tutoring, mentoring, staffing food pantries, working in homeless shelters, helping the needy in general, and very many others.

As I have emphasized, humans are social in nature with very few exceptions. Other people can augment one's life. For example, it is not unusual for a spouse to state after the death of the other that "a part of me died too." Loving and helping others adds richly to the meaning of one's own life.

Far Eastern thought repeatedly confirms this view that the main ingredient in happiness (or the equivalent of the meaning of life for it) is not materialism but "the quality of our romantic bonds, the health of our families, the time we spend with good friends, the connections we feel to communities," according to Professor Dacher Keltner in *Born to Be Good: The Science of a Meaningful Life,* page 13.

I must reiterate and emphasize here that the other person can always refuse for a variety reasons to have a relationship of high quality with you as it is her own choice. You cannot control the response of others to construct the meaning of your life the way want it; you can only try to have good relationships.

Another person can treat you as meaningless (in the sense of "lacking meaning") by neglecting, abusing, or excessively using you. People frequently disappoint and even anger each other. *You need to stop any diminishing of your meaning caused by another person as fast as you can. Too much of one's self should not be given away with insufficient return made.* (Please re-read now about quality relationships as a source of meaning, Sections 11–14.)

B. FULFILLING WORK IS A BIG PART OF THE MEANING OF LIFE

Jobs are obviously another major part of the meaning of our lives because they take up most of our energy and waking time. Our jobs need to be meaningful (in the sense of "fulfilling") so that we will not have dullness and deficiency taking up much of our lives. All workers need more meaning from work than only paychecks that support them and their nuclear families. A meaningful job would be doing work that a person cares about, matches her skills, and benefits others. It is the good that you do for yourself, your family, and others with the largest part of your life. (Please re-read now Sections 19–20 on work as a source of meaning.)

Above all, meaningful work coincides with a person's main interests in life, but many people lack these.

C. MATERIALISM IS A NEEDED BUT SMALL
PART OF THE MEANING OF LIFE

Many people today live as if materialism were the main meaning of life. It is definitely a part of it because it enables a person to survive which is our first requirement if we are to make meaning. *Possessions are a means to one's survival, but they should never be taken as an end or goal in themselves.* We can say that materialism brings "peace of body" but not "peace of mind." The gaping inadequacy and futility with materialism is that it cannot satisfy our mind's need to have more meaning than matter. Possessions soon leave feelings of emptiness, boredom, and coldness. Owning things is not even a prerequisite for making meaning. Gandhi and Thoreau owned almost nothing and led highly meaningful lives. *Even if a materialist claims that her mind does not "bother" her, she still suffers from not developing it, particularly its reflective and problem-solving capacities.*

Periods of affluence often bring mindlessness and moral corruption, as in the fall of Rome due mostly to the weakness of its leaders who were the wealthiest in the world then. The fall of many later empires east and west closely follows this pattern. So do individuals.

Recent studies show that more possessions and money make little difference to a person after she has reached a certain amount that is far less than extravagant. (Please re-read now Sections 33–34 on material possessions as a source of meaning.)

D. IDEAS OUGHT TO GUIDE THE MEANING OF LIFE.

Ideas (concepts or thoughts) as weak as they are in us, are our only reliable way to solve problems and to know truths, including even the meaning of one's life and great intangible truths. We all need to think as hard as we can to make the most of our lives. The typical person may have little inclination or interest in ideas, but the ones about the meaning of life are not complex or advanced; they concern mostly what ought to be a person's purposes in daily life. Once again, this starts on the level of common sense. (See Section 8.)

One's ideas ought then to be combined in logically sound ways in that they follow all the laws of deduction, which they usually do automatically. (See Appendix I.)

We ought to aim for creative (new, at least to a thinker) and imaginative ideas, as artists do. (See Sections 21–24.) The greatest ideas are intangibles, of course. (See Diagram 2 for examples.)

One advantage of using ideas is that they allow us to explore possibilities without risking doing actions that may have bad physical consequences that cannot be undone.

Ideas tell us how we can think about anything. Above all, they plunge deeply into intangibles instead of dwelling on the surface of things as escapes, materialism, and blind faiths do. Ideas can enlighten us about even profound truths about beauty, truth, and goodness. (See Section 35 for examples.)

Only ideas can conquer, with a huge personal effort, one's strongest emotions, subconscious desires, weak will, and anxieties that constantly threaten to lead us into mental disorder and meaninglessness (in the sense of "lack of meaning"). Our strongest ideas are not always "slaves to our passions," as modern philosopher David Hume put it. As Cohen in his *Reason and Nature* eloquently paraphrased philosopher John Locke, our reasoning may be a pitiful candle in a vast sea of darkness, but we have nothing better, and woe to whoever tries to put it out.

Some examples of guiding ideas, in alphabetical order, that can help us make meaning include the following: beauty, duty, education, goodness, happiness, honor, justice, knowledge (not mere information or data), love, pleasure, time, truth, and wisdom.

Ideas used in reasoning best guide one's own life and one's plans about increasing meaning for others and oneself. Thinking about an idea for its own sake is quite advanced, but it has hitherto distracted almost all scholars and philosophers from thinking and writing about meaning. Alack!

Thinking about the meaning of life starts the attainment of it on our firmest foundation of reasoning. Yet, *a person should not neglect implementing her ideas about the meaning of life into physical practice.* Remember to emphasize that the main part of the definition of "meaning" is someone's "impact" or effect on the material world. (See Section 2.)

E. SUMMARY: A DEFINITION OF THE MEANING OF LIFE

The following summarizes my definition of the meaning of life by combining its main sources: *the meaning of life is (=) having high-quality relationships of helping and loving others as much as you can, working at a fulfilling job, having enough material possessions, being guided by sound and creative ideas, and being very engaged in achievable goals that increase meaning for others and yourself.*

In short, *my definition calls for a person to live life deeply in several of the main sources of meaning, especially high quality relationships. Most unfortunately, a person has little control over the responses of others to her in a relationship.*

This definition gives us many worthwhile and attainable purposes.

I myself have followed it fairly well, particularly by developing the idea of meaning in general, but also by teaching philosophy to young adults, being engaged in achievable social goals, living comfortably and participating in much culture and art. The biggest lack of meaning in my life has been that most of the people with whom I had to associate are not much driven by meaning and the philosophy of life. (See Section 14.)

61

IMPLICIT VERSUS
EXPLICIT MEANING

We next need to study the history of thinking about the meaning of life to learn about it from other people beside myself. There has been very little written about meaning other than on words (see end of Section 2), but some books have recently been written about the meaning of life from the philosophical and psychological viewpoints.

I emphasize that *the meaning of life was not explicitly discussed much until 1946* when psychologist Viktor Frankl briefly did so in *Man's Search for Meaning*. (I will discuss his book in Section 67.)

I also emphasize that *it is controversial whether or not philosophies implying (= not saying this phrase, but much oriented toward it) the meaning-of-life question should count with those that address this question explicitly (literally). My own position is that the implied philosophies of the meaning of life definitely should not be so counted* because they do not make meaning itself central and explain it. Implicit philosophies of it do not even mention the phrase "the meaning of life," *but merely discuss what their authors consider most important and hence meaningful in our lives.* (See Section 3 on how "importance" or "significance" is a major sense of "meaning.") A summary of these views must guess which ideas of a philosopher's difficult writings best represent this. Of course, a guess about this can be wrong, but there is much consensus among historians of philosophy about what are the main ideas of most major philosophers, even the most erudite and dense ones.

I will next summarize in a very abbreviated way the main thinkers and eras for their views on the implied meaning of life.

Socrates

62

THE IMPLIED MEANING OF LIFE TO SOCRATES: EXAMINE LIFE

Socrates was the first thinker to implicitly realize the importance of the meaning of life. The way in which he did this was to walk around Athens in the late fourth century BCE asking anyone broad thought-provoking questions, for examples, about the virtues (good personality traits), piety, and especially the good life. He did this to get people to examine their basic beliefs and to draw out their own ideas on them. As he famously summarized his own ideas in his *Apology* (in which he was not saying he was sorry, but defending his philosophical way of life), "*The unexamined life is not worth living.*" This sounds rather harsh on people who are not gifted intellectually, but it gives excellent advice for everyone else. He told the Athenians that *they should care only about their inner selves.* All other goods would follow from doing this, he assured us.

In his questioning, Socrates recognized the great importance of living a good life. Yet, he did not develop major sources of making meaning such as God, art, and free will, plus he treated only a little the basic philosophical fields of theory of knowledge and the nature of reality (metaphysics). A developed philosophy of the meaning of life should include all these areas. In the end, Socrates produced little more than the start of an ethics of being virtuous, *but he did start in a passionate yet implied way the search for the meaning of life, mostly as the ethical good.*

It is well known that Socrates died from drinking hemlock poison inflicted by an Athenian jury because he would not give up his questioning. *His execution made making meaning a highly dramatic life-or-death matter.* (See Section 7.) *He chose death over not being able to continue his implied quest for the meaning of life.* He thereby got philosophy and the search for the implied meaning of life off to a fine start!

Socrates bequeathed to the world the critical spirit of questioning beyond facades in the personal and social realms. Our schools still largely fail to instil this.

63

THE IMPLIED MEANING OF LIFE TO PLATO: KNOWING INTANGIBLE IDEAS

Socrates much inspired a brilliant and even dazzling student named Plato who dedicated his life to the vindication of his teacher's ideas. Plato was so outraged at the execution of Socrates by the government of Athens that he almost despaired of finding justice and even meaning on earth. He eventually decided that these reside in a realm of perfect Ideas. (Recall that I capitalize this word because Plato conceived them existing external to our minds which differs much from what this word denotes today.) He emphasized the Ideas that are the greatest values: justice, beauty, truth, and especially goodness. We ought to organically "participate" (be a living part of) these Ideas as best that we can. For him, we need to live or dwell in the grand Ideas to maximize the meaning of our lives and societies, according to writer Karen Armstrong in *The Case for God, pages 64-69.* (See an example in the second paragraph below.)

Plato maintained that even physical things like a bed reflect the Idea of a perfect bed. This extreme view is not relevant to making meaning, fortunately.

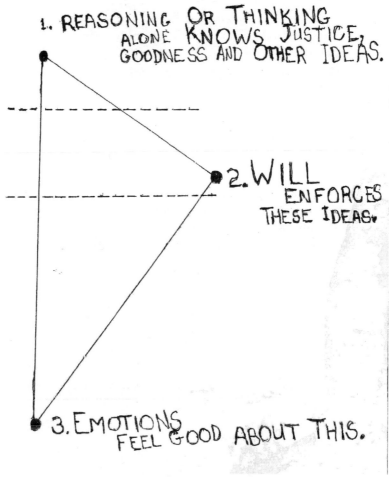

Diagram 4: Plato on What Is a Good or Balanced Individual

As a great lover of mathematics, *Plato answered all philosophical questions by finding the proper geometrical proportions of an Idea.* (See Section 16 on how the above diagram can be readily applied to his account of a just community.) For example (see Diagram 4), his answer to the question of what is a just individual can be represented by a triangle. In this diagram, a person's tiny power of thinking or reasoning ought to predominate because it alone can know what is just. Secondly, her more powerful or larger will (desire) in the second angle should enforce these ideas. Thirdly, her largest and strongest faculty of the appetites or what we today call "the emotions" ought to feel good about doing all this in the biggest third angle.

We need to think similarly about all the other Ideas (especially the great values) to know their harmonies and proper proportions so that we can apply them to our daily lives. To do this, like his teacher Socrates, Plato urged us to turn our souls or what we today call our "selves" inward away from the physical world toward knowing the Ideas.

Plato's allegory (a story in which things symbolize ideas) of the cave (see Diagram 2) excellently depicts his conception of the meaning of life in a graphic way. This allegory likens all humans to chained prisoners in a dark cave. Each prisoner needs to break her chains to escape to the greater world (realm) of Ideas outside the cave. There she needs to learn about each Idea, culminating in the Good (his equivalent of God in *The Republic*) symbolized by the blinding sun. Plato required anyone who escapes from the cave to go back down to tell the prisoners about the greater realities outside it.

Thus, I interpret *the implied Platonic meaning of life is to be highly intelligent, virtuous, socially engaged to transcend the material world*. He developed his vision far beyond Socrates' ethics and life-or-death questioning into a broad vision of all the major areas of life. Yet, his vision is too otherworldly and intellectual for the typical person. His dialogues more and more began to address not her, but his colleagues and students in his school of philosophy, the Academy. This increasing professionalization of philosophy in schools and colleges would eventually ruin it for the typical person, as it continues to do today. Plato, nevertheless, made the lasting contribution that knowing intangible Ideas can tell us the full meaning of life. However, he failed to tell us in a clear way what this is and how to live it.

64

THE IMPLIED MEANING OF LIFE TO ARISTOTLE: FULFILLMENT, THE GOLDEN MEAN AND HAPPINESS

Aristotle

Plato's brightest student Aristotle was far more down-to-earth than his esteemed teacher. Similar to his teacher, the student believed in high ideals and deep values, but he always grounds them in nature or the physical world (except for his realm of the "unmoved mover" or God), not in intangible Ideas. His book that most closely implies the meaning of life is his *Nicomachean Ethics*, named after his son. In it *Aristotle emphasized that the end goal or purpose—which term is the main sense of "meaning of life" (see Section 3, #3) for a human is to actualize her greatest potentials.* For him, this consists of having the virtues (good personal qualities or traits of a person's character).

To Aristotle, realizing the highest human potential is to actualize the intellectual virtue of contemplation (deep thinking)—after all, he himself was a philosopher! Our second greatest potential, according to him, is having the moral virtues with the main ones being temperance, courage, and justice. He elaborated that a human can build a moral character by practicing good habits to acquire these virtues. We can call his view of the actualization of one's greatest potentials, especially contemplation and the moral virtues, "*fulfillment*."

For the second part of the implied meaning of life, Aristotle argued that all virtuous actions reside in what we call "the golden mean" or the middle between two extremes, but rarely symmetrical (50-50 per cent), in every case. For example, a courageous act lies between the extremes of foolhardiness (too much) and cowardice (too little). We need to figure out the right balance of the two opposing factors in each circumstance under question. On this point, he is close to Plato's doctrine of proper proportions without his teacher's love of geometry. Their view on this is called "the Greek ideal" of attaining a proper balance (moderation) of each virtue in all of a person's actions.

The third part of Aristotle's implied meaning of life is his account of what we call "*happiness.*" He himself called this highly ambiguous word "living well." To him, doing this involves satisfying our three basic needs (as opposed to wants): (1) bodily health, (2) moderate wealth, and (3) the unlimited goods of the self (called the "soul" then) particularly love, friendship, self-esteem, honor, and aesthetic (artistic) enjoyment. Aristotle added that a person needs to have good luck in both her birth status and environment to have a happy life. (He probably would have added the right times, unlike the present age.) He would not use the word "happiness" as we do now to refer to mere moments when a person feels good as, for example, when she gets anything that she wants. Rather, he used this word to describe only a person's life as a whole.

Aristotle's implied meaning of life thus consists of fulfillment, the golden mean, and happiness. He turned away from Plato's broad vision of the Ideas. Aristotle was far more concerned, as Plato increasingly had become, with minute analysis rather than the big picture of the meaning of it all. This turn also contrasts much with Socrates' constant questioning, which he so dramatically urged by his own dying for it. (Aristotle once fled reputably stating, "I will not let Athens sin twice against philosophy.") Philosophy would become more and more a sedentary study in which typical people could scarcely find their daily lives and could little comprehend its difficult prose.

Accordingly, I will no longer summarize individual great thinkers—there were few of them until the late seventeenth century—on the implied meaning of life in their philosophies, just the main historic periods overall on this topic.

65

THE IMPLIED MEANING OF LIFE IN THE MIDDLE AGES: FAITH IN GOD

God was the overriding implied meaning of life during the entire medieval (middle) ages after the conversion of Roman emperor Constantine to Christianity in 313 until the modern period in the late seventeenth century. *Christians during those times believed that the meaning of life consists entirely of having blind faith in God.* The popularized—Jesus' teachings are actually "hard sayings"—message of the Christian God offered eternal happiness if a person just believed in him. (See Section 25 on blind faith in God.) How can there be a more rewarding, easy, and appealing meaning of life than this offer? Almost everyone in Europe, even some of its greatest thinkers, had blind faith in the Christian God. Few arguments for the existence of God were even offered during the entire Middle Ages. I have previously summarized the strongest ones that survived the onslaught of science: Thomas Aquinas' very brief arguments in the thirteenth century for a divine creator and for a grand designer of the universe. (See Section 27.)

Who needs complex arguments when they already have an easy, highly optimistic, and maximally meaningful, even if strictly subjective, answer? Yet, it is extremely unlikely that God would eternally reward anyone who made so little effort as telling God that she is sorry for her sins especially if God is just (fair) to others. If God is merciful to everyone, then it does not matter how a person lives. The awful title character in Tolstoy's *Death of Ivan Illych* is saved when he commits to God's love just before his "typical and therefore terrifying" death. Such is the distressing legacy of the Middle Ages when virtually all making meaning rested on blind faith in God.

66

THE IMPLIED MEANING OF LIFE IN
THE MODERN ERA: MATERIALISM

The religious view on the meaning of life did not change until the seventeenth century when in the Renaissance the rebirth of interest in the physical world flourished for the first time since ancient Greece and Rome. The Catholic Church had become institutional, authoritative, and corrupt in its tremendous earthly power. People began to return to their roots in the material world. The economy was finally developed, although colonialism and slavery were rampant. (These still exist in less obvious forms today.) The main intellectual interest became developing the natural sciences rather than building the tallest cathedral—which might collapse on its workers!

The revolutionary scientific method started with Leonardo da Vinci's experiments on the swinging pendulum of Galileo whom the Church made recant for his having proved that the earth revolves around the sun. This method, especially as applied by Charles Darwin to evolution, eventually destroyed the medieval blind faith in God as the sole source of meaning because science requires that all knowledge be confirmed by physical facts. So *meaning gradually came to be only what can be physically proven. This eventually resulted in widespread materialism in both* its metaphysical and ethical senses.

The modern era was the first time in western history that all individuals could afford mass-produced possessions. Ideas such as God became widely considered unprovable. (These also became what students today commonly complain are "abstract" and "boring.") Modernists in general made exceptions to believe only optimistic and flattering ideas such as free will—see Section 45 on the meaning of being free or caused—and blind faith in God—see Sections 25 and 65). The typical person became consumed with acquiring material possessions as the main meaning of life. (See Section 33 on materialism.)

170

By the end of the nineteenth century, the modern era had lost most meaning other than materialism, often combined by the typical person with a more rational faith in God from the creator and design arguments for God's existence (see Section 27).

67

BREAKTHROUGH: FRANKL ON THE SEARCH FOR MEANING

The idea of the meaning of life languished in materialism well into the twentieth century. After the horrific First World War, philosophers such as A. J. Ayer and Moritz Schlick declared that the very phrase "the meaning of life" is "meaningless" (and "nonsense") because it could not be physically verified by the sciences.

The Second World War was even more horrific than the first, so much so that it produced an effect opposite to denying meaning: the book *Man's Search for Meaning* (1946) by Viktor Frankl explicitly affirmed meaning as the key to a person's survival and quality of life. (See start of Section 60.) This book mostly studies the psychological effects on prisoners in the Nazi concentration camps at Auschwitz such where he was imprisoned. From these, he developed a brief theory of psychotherapy.

Frankl thus wrote quite little on the meaning of life itself. However, just his book's title and the shocking revelations of the attempted genocide of the Jews by the Nazis may well explain the fact that his book has sold over ten million copies and ranks as one of the ten most influential books in the United States. The title *Man's Search for Meaning* alone is so inspiring that it could account for much of the book's popularity. It finally made "meaning" explicit to the public.

Frankl's main point is that *meaning is our most important aspect* presumably because it gives a person a sense of purpose, even during her worst suffering. He observed that those who survived the concentration camp did so because they have meaning in their lives (in the sense of their "purposes or goals"), not their physical strength (no examples given). He stated that "human life . . . never ceases to have a meaning," presumably in the sense of "relationships,"in *Man's Search for Meaning, 1984 edition, page 104)*. He also stated that "man's search for meaning is the primary motivation in his life," page 121).

Frankl identified *the will to meaning, especially to find one's purpose in life, as the basic drive in humans* (which he may have derived from Nietzsche's notion of the will to power). For him, there is not one meaning in life for all people, but meaning is "unique and specific" to each person (pages 130-131). However, he did assert the cliché that love is the highest meaning for everyone without defining this very ambiguous term (page 57). Frankl concluded that the post–World War II society has the "collective neurosis" of "nihilism . . . (which) can be defined as being [existing?] has no meaning" (page 152). (See Section 53 on nihilism.)

This is all that Frankl explicitly wrote about the meaning of life, but *at last a thinker had explicitly recognized its importance in the title of a much needed and timely book. In fact, both the title of Frankl's book and his content revolve more around meaning than the meaning of life, but in a woefully undeveloped way.*

68

CRITICISMS OF MAN'S SEARCH FOR MEANING:

In general, *very little that Frankl argued about the meaning of life can be verified in any way. He made many overgeneralizing and oversimplifying statements.* For example, his statement that the will to meaning is our basic drive overlooks the fact that humans rarely even say the word "meaning." How then can it be our primary motivation? Is it explicit or implicit in us? Presumably the latter, but this is much weaker. (See Section 60.) Frankl does not say what the meaning of life is except tritely that it is "love" or maybe "purpose." Or is he suggesting that every person needs to find their own meaning of life? This does not much help me know the meaning of my life. He did not address such huge issues, for examples, as ought (prescriptive) meaning be mostly subjective or objective, relative or absolute, and materialistic or divine. Nor does he even define "the meaning of life" or "meaning". This causes much confusion regarding what he is trying to express. Thus, *his views on the meaning of life are suggestive, but quite undeveloped and incomplete.* They are rather superficial, but at least they made an explicit start to develop this woefully neglected idea.

Frankl deserves much credit for his courage in presenting such a big idea to the public. He did so at a time when it was looking for new ideas to overcome the atrocious evils done in World War II. He also deserves credit for being the first person to explicitly write even a little about the meaning of life for a large audience.

69

THE CURRENT ERA: MORE BOOKS ON THE MEANING OF LIFE

Frankl's book finally opened the door a little to explicitly discussing the meaning of life. Since its publication, the main development in the meaning of life is that *books and anthologies (collections of short writings) on this topic were published at an almost yearly rate starting in 1981*. Most of these books are popular, but some (especially German) are scholarly. Philosophers and psychologists, some prominent, wrote them. I will next very briefly summarize some main points of a few of the most important these works in chronological order.

Before Frankl's book, *The Meaning of Meaning* (1923) by professors C. K. Ogden and I. A. Richards sounds as if it would be directly about the meaning of life, but it almost entirely covers only the meaning of symbols and words or language, a topic which I stated that I would not cover. (See end of Section 3.) This book has a quite scholarly—and therefore unhelpful!—chapter on the philosophical meaning of life. At least "meaning" finally appeared in the title of a book—twice! So sad that this book is almost entirely about symbols and words, not our lives! The search for the meaning of life did not begin with it.

The next important book on the meaning of life is an anthology appropriately titled *The Meaning of Life* (1981), finely edited by professor of philosophy E. D. Klemke. This collection of nineteen articles were originally published in philosophical and theological books and journals. It starts with the debate about whether or not the meaning of life is found in the traditional conception of God. The majority of the articles on this debate answer no. Next is a section on the question, "Does the current secular way of life have meaning?" The majority of articles on this question answer yes. The final section of articles examines whether or not the question itself about life's meaning makes sense. They all answer yes.

Professor Thomas Nagel's *What Does It All Mean?* (1987) is a 101-page textbook for introduction to philosophy courses, which obviously needs to be supplemented by other texts because of its small size. All his chapters are actually about traditional philosophical questions except the one on knowing whether or not other minds exist which is a long way from finding the meaning of life! Only his last chapter concerns this topic by dealing with the absurd. Nagel provocatively concludes that, "Perhaps we have to put up with being ridiculous. Life may not be only meaningless but absurd" (page 101). Neither a pleasant nor a pretentious prospect! At least he is one of the few current philosophers to take such nontraditional ideas as ridiculousness, absurdity, and the meaning seriously, but he seems to be using the title largely to sell his textbook except for his short last chapter!

Professor Irving Singer wrote a trilogy of acclaimed books about love, but he received little attention when he published *Meaning in Life: The Creation of Value* (1992). In this book he naturally made love the meaning of life. He requires that when a person's love creatively helps another and this person is happy, she has meaning in her life. Singer concludes that "the meaning of life is the life of meaning" (page 148). He focuses only on an individual's quest for meaning, but he thereby has the biggest implied interest in making meaning of all the books on the meaning of life.

In 1996 writer and editor of *Tikkun* magazine Rabbi Michael Lerner started a small movement for meaning with *The Politics of Meaning*. His Foundation for Ethics and Meaning held summits in at least seven U.S. cities, but none were sustained for long. (Did they all soon become disillusioned after they were initially inspired by politics?) As the title of his book indicates, Lerner approaches meaning from the political perspective, although he does not define any terms. Nor does meaning play a large role in his big book. He does sharply criticize how democracy and capitalism in their current forms in the U. S. deprive its inhabitants of meaning because they unjustly force them to work too long and hard to make meaning outside their jobs.

Lerner attempts "to restore hope in our cynical age" about politics. He proposes ten "progressive," that is, quite liberal, steps to do this. His concern is far more with politics than it is with the meaning of life or his avowed meaning in politics.

Writer Julian Baggini has attained a little notoriety as editor of *The Philosophers' Magazine* for a general audience. The title of his *What's It All About?* (2004)comes from the title of a popular song in the British film *Alfie* (1966). His answer to the meaning-question is, like Lerner's political solution, populist. Baggini much agrees with the simple vision of it stated in Monty Python's absurdist movie *The Meaning of Life* (1983): "try to be nice to people, avoid eating fat, read a good book every now and then, get some walking in, and try to live together in peace and harmony," quoted on page 185. Like Frankl and Singer,

Baggini tritely maintains that undefined love provides most of the meaning of life. His book is written in easily comprehensible style, as all books on this topic should be because it concerns everyone.

A few other books explicitly on the meaning of life have been published recently with much agreement on main ideas. This is much more than had been done in previous centuries, as my historical sketch shows. Yet, none of these books have had much effect on us except Frankl's. Society today continues to mostly ignore the idea of the meaning of life.

70

CONCLUSIONS: BROADENING TRUTHS AND MAKING MEANING NOW

The current era of extreme relativism, materialism (both ethical and metaphysical), and seemingly endless, almost worldwide economic recession is the right time to start to apply the developed ideas of meaning and the meaning of life to the daily concerns of the typical person. Reflective and engaged people seek effective responses to these current deplorable conditions by making meaning for others and themselves.

We can always know more about meaning and how to live more meaningful lives, just as we can about God. (See Section 25 on rational faith.) *The meaning-question has no final answer as many people assume that it does. Instead, it has ever-broadening answers and ideas that enable us to know and make more meaning.* A person can get more of the total truth about the great questions, but never the whole of it. This is an optimal condition for humans because it gives us broader answers that help us make more meaning without feeling complacent.

This question about how we can know in general big truths about intangibles, especially meaning and the meaning of life, is the most meaningful (in the sense of "fundamental") one of all philosophy, because you must first know how you know big truths. Let us call this "the truth-question." Like the meaning-question (Section 1) and the God-question (Section 25), we can always know more about such big truths, but never the judicial "whole truth and nothing but the truth". Yet, the more that a person knows about such matters, whether for or against their existence, she gets more of or closer to the big truths. We ought not regard such big truths to have simple "true" or "false" answers, as many of us were taught in grade school to do for much simpler questions. We live and die for the big truths about the meaning of it all such as God, justice, respect and truth. (See Sections 7 and 37.) Thus, in approaching the meaning-question, we ought to first study the truth-question and the nuances of knowing life's big truths in the branch of philosophy known as "epistemology."

Yet, it is appalling how few people even raise the truth-question, like the God-question. (See Section 25.) Today the vast majority of people assume that the only way that we can know truths is by means of sensory experience, in particular by sight (including reading). Philosophers call this relatively new (since the late eighteenth century) epistemology "empiricism." However, this simple epistemology causes the very problem of knowing intangibles because we obviously cannot experience any of them directly.

I myself have proposed intuitions tested by making more meaning are the way we can know big truths about meaning. (See Sections 38-39.) The reader is encouraged to develop her own ways to know these truths. We must maintain a healthy skepticism to continue the develop the idea of meaning. After all, as Francis Bacon quipped, "Knowledge is power." Since meaning is the greatest and highest knowledge, it can give its knower the greatest power. (See Section 40.)

Why not *leave a legacy of maximum meaning*, especially for your children and friends? (Celebrity Oprah Winfrey seriously calls this for a female "a lega-she.") Leaving only a materialistic one, especially money, rarely lasts long. More meaningful by far is a legacy of people modeling the mostly intangibles meaning made in your life, for examples, your virtues, aging well, joy, openness, and love of life. These are the birthrights of everyone.

Why not *live a life of depth by plunging deeply into making meaning*? You do not need to go far to find shallow people who live only on the materialistic surface of life and cannot conceive of anything beyond the concrete or physical. How sad! No one really wants to be a shallow person. *Seeking and making meaning in life engages a person fully and deeply in the best that life has to offer us.*

Velasquez writes that we tend to think about the meaning of life only when death enters our lives (*Philosophy, 2014 edition, page 618*), but then it is too late to make more meaning. Alas! (See Section 31 on how affirmatively answering the God-question at death is also too late.)

Let us make the most meaning that we can now! Why not make today your most meaningful one yet mostly by drawing from its many sources, starting now? (As they used to say, "Go, man, go!" Also, as they used to say in a religious context, "Amen! Amen! Be it so! Be it so!" Ha! Ha!)

I hope that this book will help you make more meaning for others and yourself. What could be deeper, better or more?

APPENDIX I

SOME BASIC LAWS OF LOGIC

We all obviously need to know how to think well or logically. Logic (=) studies *the laws for sound thinking.* There is only one logic in the strict sense (see Section 51, #2) for all people. *Logic has many laws for correct thinking. By knowing these laws, a person can test every instance of thinking to determine its soundness (= strength because it does not break any of the laws of logic).*

Logic is a branch of philosophy developed to correct thinking about basic beliefs and values. Aristotle amazingly thought of much of its basics in several treatises (small books) on the subject.

Logic gives us an objective way to tell whether any thinking is strong or weak. (See again Section 51, #2 on the objectivity of logic.) More knowledge and use of it would lessen much of the today's subjective thinking, especially extreme relativism. (See Sections 47–48 on mostly subjective meaning and 56–57 on extreme relativism.) *The laws of logic can provide a much-needed standard to test especially our thinking about non-factual matters such as opinions, judgments and values. These make* up an extremely large *and important part of our thinking.*

The laws of logic are prescriptive because they tell us how we should or ought to think. (See Section 4.) *Because they are this, these laws give us a solid and universal standard on which to judge all thinking, as I hope that I have done throughout this book.* These laws are particularly helpful for evaluating opinions which is what we think of when we philosophize and what we engage in much other thinking.

These laws can teach us how to think better and to communicate more clearly. However, because of the complexity of human thinking, *we do not always know how to apply the laws of logic definitely or correctly and whether or not a particular one applies.*

The following are some of the more helpful laws of logic to evaluate the soundness of all our thinking:

1. ARGUMENTS IN GENERAL:

The *first law* of logical thinking: always organize your thinking in "*arguments*" which are its smallest unit. This word is in quotation marks because logic uses it in a special sense (see Section 2 on defining meaning), not as "disagreements," but (=) "reasons given to show that a belief is true." In logic these reasons are called "premises." They offer support for the belief or point to be proven in each argument called "the conclusion." When a person organizes her thinking into arguments she uses her evidence as premises to back up her conclusion that she argues is true. We must be very careful that the premises in an argument are true according to logic: we can know that facts are true by means of induction and the scientific method; opinions by deduction and other laws of logical reasoning. (See Main Types of Logical Arguments next.)

DIAGRAM 5—structure of a logical argument:
>   Because of a premise (evidence)
>   And because of another premise (other evidence)
>   Therefore, a conclusion follows soundly

This diagram is usually too mechanical and complicated for everyday thinking and argumentation, but it expresses the underlying structure or form of a logical argument.

MAIN TYPES OF LOGICAL ARGUMENTS:

1. INDUCTION = a logical argument based on physical experiences and observations. They reason from particular experiences (often called "cases" or "examples") as premises to a generalization about them in the conclusion. Example: This swan is white, that swan is white, and those swans are white (premises); therefore, all swans are white (conclusion). In a sound induction in which all its laws have been followed the conclusion only probably follows as true because one's experiences can be contradicted by later experiences, as for example, black swans were discovered in Australia.

All the natural and social sciences use induction because it makes experiments and observations to think logically about the world and people respectively. We ought to use inductions to think logically about facts in general.

2. DEDUCTION = logical arguments using only thinking. They reason from generalizations used as premises to a more particular conclusion about them. Example: All men are mortal and Socrates is a man (premises). Therefore, Socrates is mortal (conclusion). The conclusion of a sound deduction follows with necessity, not just probability as inductions do, because deductions consist only of sheer thinking, not experiencing things with one's senses. Deduction expresses only patterns about the abstract relationships among ideas and classes of things in an argument. So, a deduction is either correct (called "valid" in logic) or not. An invalid deductive argument does not correctly relate or think about ideas or classes of things according to the proper laws especially transitivity (if one idea is related to a second idea and the second is related to the third, then the first is related to the third) which is the basis of deduction. The premises in a deduction are assumed to be true, but they should be critically examined before they are accepted as premises.

The fields of philosophy and mathematics use only deduction. Deduction is rather theoretical and does not improve thinking much, but it gives us objective laws to test our thinking and helps us understand our pure thinking. However, we can use it fruitfully to test all our opinions for their validity.

2. DEFINITIONS:

An area of logic that much helps good thinking and communicating is the logic of language (words). An important topic in this area is defining words. *Its first law is the following: always define any unfamiliar or ambiguous word as soon as you use it.* To "define" a word is (=) to "specify exactly what it refers to" or, etymologically, "to set boundaries" on what it designates.

Always define a word the way that most people use it (as found in a dictionary) or make it very clear whenever you use a word in one of its special senses. (See Section 2 on defining "meaning.")Many words, for example, "strike," have dozens of legitimate senses, but most words have only one definition.

Do not define—or even use—words that are strongly negative or positive in their emotional suggestions unless these are warranted by the case. Example: You are "stubborn" (negative emotional suggestion), but I am "firm" (positive). Otherwise, *use neutral or unemotional words.*

To define a word, first put it in its proper general class that it shares with similar things, for example, "humans" are classified with "animals." The father of logic, Aristotle, called the general class of a definition its "genus." Then put the word in the specific class in which it differs from all others in its general class; for example, humans are "rational" animals. Aristotle called this a definition's "specific difference." His definition of "humans" as "rational animals" still holds today despite Freud's emphasis on the subconscious.

3. CRITICAL AND CREATIVE THINKING:

Another branch of the laws of logic is to think critically (=) "find faults or weaknesses with beliefs and ideas." All beliefs can be criticized to some extent.

Even opposite ideas have a degree of truth, for example, humans are good versus humans are bad, so the truth of opposing ideas is limited by the other. Specifying (qualifying) the exact extent to which a belief holds is essential to critical thinking. *Always be as specific as you can* because this makes your thinking more concrete. *Giving examples makes a general idea specific and concrete.*

Criticizing or finding fault with arguments needs to be done before a person engages in her own positive thinking. It helps your own constructive thinking if you first have a critical attitude. Critical thinking fosters developing and sharpening one's thinking ability.

Thinking can consist of *creative* or new ideas or thoughts, at least for you. You are creative whenever you solve a problem because you then have to think of a new idea to overcome an existing blockage of a solution. Creative ideas reside in your pre- or subconscious. A good way to help these come out is to incubate ("hatch") them by sleeping on a problem for a night or doing something similar to give the subconsciousness more time to be creative. Write creative ideas as soon as you can so that you do not forget them as they do not fit in easily with your other beliefs. Not many rules can be given for this branch of logic because as creative it constantly makes new ones! (See Section 21 for more on creativity and the imagination in the arts.)

4. FALLACIES

(=) "wrong ways or patterns of thinking." A fallacy does not correctly connect premises to their conclusion because it breaks at least one of the many laws of logic. *You can disprove an argument if you know that it commits a fallacy. A fallacious argument is weak and so should not be accepted or believed to be true.*

EXAMPLES of frequent fallacies in arguments:

popular appeal = a conclusion or statement is true because many people believe it;

appeal to pity = something is sad if a conclusion is true;

contradiction = denies in the conclusion what it asserts in the premises, usually in different words; and

name-calling = calling someone a derogatory (bad) name instead of giving a reason that disputes her argument.

There are many more types of fallacies! No one has counted them all.

SUMMARY OF LOGIC: Logic gives us prescriptive laws to know how to think well and organize our thinking starting with using premises (evidence) to a conclusion (the point) in an "argument (a unit of thinking)." Inductive arguments show which physical observations are true, whereas deductive ones concern only the validity (proper relationships) of reasoning about ideas and classes of things in an argument.

The logic of language teaches us how we ought to use words for communicating, especially by carefully defining any unclear or vague term.

The rules of definitions tell us how to properly classify or categorize a word so that it is distinctive from all others. The logic of language implores us to use neutral terms unless warranted otherwise. It gives us many other objective rules for communicating in a logical way.

Critical thinking negatively examines all beliefs to determine the degree of truth of each. Creative thinking involves conceiving the highest kind of new and positive ideas. Using it is the only way to solve both theoretical and practical problems.

An argument containing a fallacy gives us a logical way to say regarding it, "That's wrong" because it breaks a law of logic in connecting premises to their conclusion. There are many types of fallacies that frequently plague our arguments and thinking.

APPENDIX II

EXAMPLES OF CLASS HAND-OUTS
ORIENTED TOWARD
MAKING MEANING

(See Section 20 on methods of teaching meaning indirectly on how these hand-outs do this in an area or problem of philosophy.)

WHAT IS HUMAN NATURE?

Human nature refers to the distinguishing traits of humans such as thinking and advanced feelings. This is a philosophical question that everyone needs to answer. Today we have largely forgotten what it means to be human, but we can recall what this is.

Motivations to learn this: Since we all must live with other humans, it will help to understand what makes a human "*tick*" (work). *Success in all your relationships and career* often depends much on how well you know what true human nature is.

Human nature has *two main senses*:

1. PRESCRIPTIVE = What is *the one key trait that all humans should* (ought to) *share?*

2. DESCRIPTIVE = What is the *one key trait that all humans actually do have?*

OPPOSITE TRAITS are embodied in a human. Are humans walking contradictions?

EXAMPLES (Be able to explain one.):

* *good* or *bad?* (Freud maintains that humans are extremely violent) DISCUSS: Are humans so evil and violent? Just a personal trauma can momentarily provoke anyone to commit severe violence.

* *rational* or *irrational* (Page 59 describes how humans often *take risky chances* even with their lives and are *easily manipulated*, for example, by advertising.)

peaceful or *warlike* (aggressive)?

transcendent or natural?

social or loner?

a*ltruistic = favors others* (example: Mother Theresa and any others _____?) or *egoists* = always *favors self?* Which of these two a person is depends on her___[intention]. More on this later . . .

IN-CLASS EXERCISE: After briefly discussing these traits in small groups, write which opposite trait in each pair that each group member thinks predominates in humans.

Does human nature even exist? This concept can be abused and used properly (know one of each):

* **ABUSES**: "Human nature" can be used to excuse *bad behaviors*, for examples, people often say, "It's human nature to be lazy (or greedy or selfish or aggressive [Freud!]) or that owning slaves is just if one's race is superior."-- (Read Aristotle's defense of it)--or _____[student's example].

* **USES**: It gives you *a broad basis to deal with humans.* Knowing what human nature is can tell you how to best *understand and relate to other people.*

The *traditional philosophy* of human nature makes several huge *assumptions:*

1. A human has an *intangible self.* This self is *the same* person throughout one's life despite many changes. The self has an intangible *mind*. This tells us our *purposes or goals*, according to Aristotle.

2. Humans have *souls* that live forever. Some people today claim that they had *after-death experiences* that prove that they have a soul because people revived from death know what happened after their bodies died. DISCUSS these claims.

3. The traditional philosophy *emphasizes our ability to reason* = to think about ideas. This philosophy holds that we *ought*—prescriptive—to be rational. (This sounds reasonable. Ha! Ha!) *Only* reason can reliably know truths. Our power to reason is quite limited, but *it can control our emotions and wants*, like the two chariot horses Plato compares this to.

Criticism: our thinking feels weak (bloodless), whereas our emotions and wants are very strong.

DIAGRAM OF HUMAN NATURE TO PLATO (Explain in your own words.): on Smartboard (See Diagram 4.)

WHAT IS ETHICS?

(This is another example of a class hand-out that I use to indirectly teach meaning about an area of philosophy, this one being ethics in general.)

Ethics = <u>evaluating</u> actions to determine whether or not they are <u>good</u> (right) or bad (wrong)

For Plato, ethics = "the study of the good." The "good" is "whatever ought —note prescription—to have <u>worth</u> in one's life." ("Ethical" and "moral" are largely synonymous.)

Traditional ethics consists mostly of <u>THEORIES</u> (interrelated ideas applicable to practice) about what is the greatest good. This good sets a <u>standard</u> (ideal) to judge whether or not any action is ethical. Examples: the most <u>useful</u> <u>results</u> (called "utilitarian ethics") and doing your <u>duty</u> (obligation) despite the results (called "duty ethics"). (Both theories will be studied soon, but they cannot decide what is good that we all can agree on.)

* Since ethics guides our lives, it is very important to have high moral standards.

* Ethics tells us what we <u>ought (should)</u> do, not what we actually do do. [Ha! Ha!] It is <u>prescriptive,</u> not descriptive.

* The greatest value in ethics is <u>the good.</u> We are all trying to find this, for examples, good jobs and friends. Ethics teaches us how to live the <u>[good]</u> life.

MORAL PROBLEMS

* You face a <u>moral problem</u> whenever you have to decide what is the good (right) action for you to do. For example, should you tell your friend that her friend is cheating and many other problems in sexual ethics such as the following examples: pre-marital and extra-marital sex, cohabitation, daily compromises in a marriage, and abortion. Each example of these individual ethical actions ought to be felt with the strong intensity that they deserve as among our most meaningful (in the sense of "important")

EXAMPLES of moral problems for individual or personal ethics: taking responsibility for your actions, laziness (not developing one's potentials), being self-centered, lying, cheating and stealing (if you don't get caught), using others, dominating discussions, polluting the environment and wasting energy--by driving your car!--, causing death to billions of sensing animals a year by eating them, pursuing wants and luxuries rather than fulfilling needs, fair pay, honest work, social activism—phew!—any others? _____

[student's example]

SOCIAL EXAMPLES OF ETHICAL PROBLEMS: We all are also involved in very many moral problems in our society. For examples: unjust wars (including nuclear), terrorism, business and medical ethics (very many problems), abortion, the death penalty, euthanasia, racial prejudice, corrupt politicians, scandals in business and engineering, and others? _____ [student's example]

Your decisions determine the values that you live by. Reflect much on them first! You actually [define] who you are as a person when you make moral decisions. A person makes a decision about an ethical problem on the basis of her _____ _____ [highest value].

WHY SHOULD I BE ETHICAL?

Temptations to be unethical are very hard to resist if you surely are not caught. By being unethical, you can get more things for yourself for free! This raises a basic question of life, "Why should I be ethical?"

DISCUSS: Would you steal a smartphone if you would not get caught? Why or why not?

* People who are unethical definitely lose __[intangibles] such as love, respect, goodness and justice. These are our basic needs, not just desires or wants, as a smartphone is.

* Another argument for being ethical comes from Plato. He argued that if you are unethical, you will become mentally unbalanced or sick because you are being ruled by your wants and emotions, not by reason. So if you hurt others, you are really *hurting yourself more.*

Our society is quite unethical. Just look at the news about racial discrimination, gangs, drug abuse, violence (glorified in the media), pollution in the environment, irresponsible businesses, constant wars and _____.

Most people are ethical only because they blindly ____[conform] to following society's standards and fear ___[getting caught]. Ethics teaches us how to solve moral problems by using our intelligence, intangible ideas, and logical reasoning.

TEACHING FOR MEANING

In this brief appendix, I will summarize, as best that I can, how I struggled for over forty years to teach philosophy in a way that has much meaning to the typical student.

Again, of course, the first question for me as I began my career teaching philosophy was, "What is meaning?" Recall that I defined "meaning" simply as the impact that a thing, person or idea has. (See Section 2.) In other words, the meaning of anything is the effect that it has on something. Also recall that in the realm of ideas, including education, "meaning" usually refers to a positive "influence" that the teaching of philosophy has on students' lives. (See Section 3.)

Even with this definition, it is not easy to know what "meaning" is. I groped at it almost daily, including week-ends, preparing and clarifying lectures on hand-outs, even ones that I have taught many times already. I knew that "meaning" has much to do with what my pseudo-rebellious generation called "relevance" during the turbulent '60's. Yet, that word turned out to largely refer to "career guidance" if we judge by how much American colleges have increasingly become the credentialing institutions for the professions. One's career certainly is a major part of a person's life, but it is far from the whole of it. One of the main reasons that I chose philosophy is that it is the only field that can study the understanding and betterment of our lives as a whole from the rational point of view.

Without any training or mentoring, I continued to grope for how philosophy could have maximum meaning for my students, almost all of whom had poor reading, writing, and thinking skills. Perhaps the main pedagogical lesson that I learned in my career is that *teaching meaning is a continuing process of determining how philosophical ideas can have an impact (influence) on a student's life.* In other words, there is no grand meaning of life, or even meaning, to be revealed by philosophy, only gradual revelations of deeper truths that allow students to live more fully, richly, purposely, and especially deeply in their awareness of more than the materialistic (physical) level of existence.

In other words, I decided that a professor of philosophy needs *to transform the totally abstract ideas of philosophy into enriched and deepened daily lives that enable students to transcend the shallow materialism of our stupid society, especially through intangible ideas and values such as goodness (for example good interests, friends, and careers), a highly developed sense of beauty in the arts, justice in relationships, free choices and many other great values.*

This transformation is not easy to make since the latter (the materialistic) is so easy to know requiring no imagination and the former (the intangible) is so obscure difficult to even conceive.

Let me explain most generally how I teach meaning in the field of the philosophy of human nature (See Appendix II for a class hand-out on a lecture/discussion on human nature.) I emphasize when I introduce this topic that *it can teach students how they can best deal with humans. I stress how their interactions can have more impact if they have their own ideas about what makes humans "tick." I offer even success in their careers if they know something about human nature that other people do not.* In economics this is called its first law of "supply and demand."

I also introduce other major issues in the philosophy of human nature such as how we embody opposing, almost contradictory, traits, for examples, good or bad, altruistic or egoistic, social or loner, peaceful or aggressive, rational or irrational, transcendent of the physical world or strictly natural, and many other opposing traits. If a student determines which of these traits in each pair dominates in us, she will know more fully what it means (in the sense of "signifies") to be human. I then have students decide their positions on each of these, along with their main reason for each, by discussing them in small groups in class and later writing them in their journals. Students in these ways come to understand the almost contradictory nature of humans to be able to deal with them more meaningfully (in the sense of "broadly") in their relationships, for example, marriage.

Finally for the example of human nature, I will discuss how I teach the self which makes up one of its main ideas, treated as meaningfully as I can. What I consider most meaningful about this idea is whether or not it truly exists as an intangible in humans. I try to impress on students how the self may be more than the brain (the philosophical question of consciousness). The main implication for meaning in this idea resides the consequent question whether or not the human mind, not brain, possesses an immortal soul. *This has tremendous meaning for students sheerly in terms of the number of years involved: less than a hundred years if humans have only a brain, whereas we are immortal (endless years) if we have a soul, just as in the God-question.* (See Section 25.) Thus, the concept of the self or soul in human nature potentially has much meaning, indeed

I will conclude this essay by developing in a little more detail than in Section 20 some pedagogic techniques that I have found particularly effective for teaching meaning, even if implicit or indirect:

1. A suitable topic for teaching meaning comes from one that can influence or impact on raising the quality of a student's life (for that is how I defined "meaning"). It cannot be too big or too theoretical. Some examples of topics that are excluded from teaching meaning include theories of justice and ethics- -and any theories themselves not applied in a specific way to a student's life!-- and deduction which still consumes most of a logic textbook. (See Appendix I on deduction.)

2. *Drawing diagrams frequently helps to teach meaning by making the abstract ideas of philosophy visible and concrete to at least some degree. This combination gives meaning,* whereas abstract ideas by themselves do not (other than themselves) because meaning comes from impacts, effects or relationships, not from isolated words. (See Section 2.)

I can spontaneously draw diagrams consisting of lines, circles, squares, triangles and other geometrical forms for almost all ideas on the blackboard or smartboard. (See Diagrams 1 and 4 for Plato on the just community and the just individual respectively.)

A diagram gives students a physical image to remember, not just another set of abstract and hence largely meaningless words. On exams I require that students be able to explain in words the ideas represented in a diagram, not just draw it.

3. *My final example of a pedagogic technique that teaches meaning is giving examples. Specific examples serve much the same purpose as drawing diagrams, namely, to give a physical embodiment or a concrete instance of an abstract idea.* Again, this satisfies the definition of "meaning." On my lecture hand-outs, I always give several examples for each major idea. My students know that on the next exam (whether essay or objective version) they need to fully explain how any one of these examples (or one of their own, which few can do) illustrates an idea to show that they fully know its meaning.

MEANING AND LIFELONG LEARNING

Lifelong learning is actually the goal of all education. Its main trait is that it must be meaningful. I here define this highly ambiguous term in general as whatever has "good or positive impact." In the realm of education, this should more specifically refer to "affirmative mental influence on a student's life and thinking." The main question here is how can we make it so? Here I will very briefly indicate how the idea of meaning help us in answering this question.

Like much else, lifelong learning must come from the assent of the individual or in pedagogic terms, be "intrinsic." If a student has a high I. Q., this is no problem because she enjoys learning as it comes easily to her. However, most students will need to be motivated. Motivation must instill a desire to learn lifelong. How to do this is the basic unanswered, perhaps unanswerable, question in all education. (See Section 16, #4.)

Reasons are quite weak at motivating students who do not give their inner consent for emotional reasons. Yet, we have many other theories of motivation, most of which are of little avail: behaviorist, incentive, push and pull, Maslow's hierarchy, drives, goal setting and cognitive dissonance. Teachers can motivate by being inspiring, but this is another complex pedagogical issue.

Perhaps the greatest motivation to lifelong learning is the maturity and leisure of the students. Professors and teachers obviously can do little about this, and thus about instilling lifelong learning in their students.

My own motivation for lifelong learning stems from my innate respect for great writers, thinkers and ideas. This motivation gave me great joy throughout my life. As Aretha Franklin put it so rhythmically, "R-e-s-p-e-c-t! Sock it to me!"

What are the chances of restoring this respect today? I myself think quite unlikely.

Conclusion: Lifelong learning has mostly subjective meaning to a student in that it pertains mostly to a student's own inner motivation.

Name Index

A

Abernethy, Bob, 98
Adams, William A., 3
Adler, Mortimer, 104, 109
Ahura Mazda, 78
Anderson, Jon, 6
Aristotle (Greek philosopher), 5–6, 9, 95, 120, 127, 137, 167–68, 183, 187
Armstrong, Karen, 164

B

Baggini, Julian, 157, 176–77
Becker, Ernest, 16
Beethoven, Ludwig van, 56–57, 97
Bergson, Henri, 17
Berman, Philip, 64
Bernini, 74
Bohm, David, 66
Bole, William, 98
Bradley, F. H., 135
Bruner, Jerome, 17
Buber, Martin, 25, 27–31, 42
Buonarroti, Michelangelo, 51, 61

C

Calder, Alexander, 52
Camus, Albert, 17–18, 141–42
Cohen, Morris R., 7, 46, 159
Constantine (emperor), 169
Copland, Aaron, 58
Cottingham, John, 156

D

Dahmer, Jeffrey, 131, 133
Darwin, Charles, 170
Descartes, Rene, 96, 145
Dewey, John, 10, 108, 137
Dostoevsky, Fyodor, 77–78, 141
Dreyfuss, Hubert, 145
Dylan, Bob, 57, 143

E

Eagleton, Terry, 156
Einstein, Albert, 95
Elgar, Edgar, 58
Elijah (Hebrew prophet), 14
Emerson, Ralph Waldo, 34

F

Feynman, Richard, 17
Finn, Huckleberry, 29
Flanagan, Owen, 156
Ford, Dennis, 3
Francis I (Pope), 145
Franck, Frederick, 75
Frankfurt, Harry, 10
Frankl, Viktor, 19, 161, 172–77
Freud, Sigmund, 14, 101, 187
Friend, David, 157

G

Gandhi, Mahatma, 101, 103–4, 153, 158

H

Hamlet (fictional character), 153
Hamlin, Hannibal, 39–40
Hansberry, Lorraine, 54–55
Hedges, Chris, 98
Hegel, Georg, 135
Heidegger, Martin, 136
Hitler, Adolph, 129, 133
Hopper, Edward, 59
Hubbell, C. Lee, 134
Hughes, Langston, 54–55

J

Jesus, 111, 153, 169
Julius Caesar (Roman emperor), 153

K

Kant, Immanuel, 6, 49, 51, 72, 91, 95, 157
Karl Marx, 34
Kazanjian, Michael M., 97
Kelly, Sean Dorrance, 145
Keltner, Dacher, 157
Kierkegaard, Soren, 141
King, Martin Luther, 55, 101
Kinnier, Richard, 7
Klemke, E. D., 175
Koenig, Alfred, 46

L

Langer, Suzanne, 17, 51, 59
Lear (fictional character), 153
Lerner, Michael, 176
Lin, Maya, 7
Lincoln, Abraham, 39, 153
Locke, John, 159
Lucas, George, 74

M

Macbeth (fictional character), 142, 153
Mandela, Nelson, 153
Mao Tse-tung, 77
Marx, Karl, 34
Mazda, Ahura, 78
Moorhead, Hugh, 104, 117
More, Thomas, 51
Moses (Hebrew prophet), 28, 75
Mother Theresa (Roman Catholic nun), 187
Mozart, Amadeus, 51, 58
Munch, Edvard, 59

N

Nagel, Thomas, 176
Naylor, Magdalena, 4, 86
Naylor, Thomas H., 4, 86
Newton, Isaac, 95
Nietzsche, Freidrich, 3, 173

O

Ogden, C. K., 175
Othello (fictional character), 153

P

Paul (apostle), 66, 75, 116
Perry, R. B., 126
Picasso, Pablo, 52, 55–56
Plato (Greek philosopher), 5–6, 36–37, 47, 60, 78, 90–92, 94–95, 100, 136, 164–68, 187–89
Plotinus (philosopher), 103
Polanyi, Michael, 16
Pollock, Jackson, 50
Prine, John, 35
Putman, Robert D., 34
Python, Monty, 176

R

Rader, Melvin, 109
Ravel, Maurice, 61
Renoir, Pierre, 58–59
Richards, I. A., 175
Rijn, Rembrandt van, 51
Robinson, D. H., 45, 57, 97
Rose, Charlie, 74
Russell, Bertrand, 136

S

Schiller, Friedrich, 57
Schindler, Oskar, 44
Schopenhauer, Arthur, 142
Shakespeare, William, 153
Shiva (deity), 50
Singer, Irving, 143, 176
Skinner, B. F., 118
Socrates (Greek philosopher), 5, 15,
     18, 81, 150, 153, 162–64, 166,
     168, 182
Stalin, Joseph, 77
Stewart, David, 66
Stocker, Wessel, 14
Stuart, Jesse, 116

T

Tchaikovsky, Pyotyr Ilyich, 58
Terkel, Studs, 44
Thomas Aquinas, Saint, 6, 72, 169
Thompson, Garrett, 142
Thoreau, H. D., 153, 158
thou (Buber), 27–28, 30–31
Tolle, Eckhard, 17
Tolstoy, Leo, 143, 169
Turkle, Sherry, 41
Twain, Mark, 29
Typper, 32

V

Van Gogh, Vincent, 61
Velasquez, Manuel, 7, 179
Vermeer, Johannes, 51

W

Warhol, Andy, 50
Whitehead, Alfred North, 136
Whitman, Walt, 34
Willimon, William H., 4, 86
Winfrey, Oprah, 179

Z

Zoroaster, 78

GENERAL INDEX

A

Abrahamic religions, 64
absolutes, 148–52
aesthetic, 48–49, 60, 168
afterlife, 64–65, 82, 84, 111
agnostics, 67, 81–82, 105
arguments, 5, 7, 10, 12, 24, 65–70, 72–81, 83, 92–93, 95–97, 119–20, 129, 135–37, 169, 182–85
  creator, 68–69, 72–73, 93
  logical, 67, 92, 182
Art Institute of Chicago, 60
artworks, 24, 48–54, 56, 58, 60–61

B

big bang, 73, 79, 149
Brothers Karamazov, The (Dostoevsky), 78

C

Categorical imperative, 91, 157
Chicago, 6, 21–22, 40, 55–56, 60, 88
Chicago Tribune, 6
choices, free, 91, 120–21, 144, 149–50, 190
City Watch (Anderson), 6
College of Complexes, 43
consciousness, 93, 95–96, 109, 137, 191
creativity, 48, 52–53, 60–61, 93, 123, 184
criticisms, 21, 78, 82, 110–11, 131, 138, 144, 147–48, 152

D

death, 11, 16, 18–19, 57, 64–65, 74, 81–83, 111, 116, 140–41, 143, 163, 169, 179, 187–89
Death of a Salesman (Miller), 156
deduction, 47, 68, 95, 159, 182–83, 191
definition of impact, 7
dreams, 54–55, 88

E

emotions, 25–26, 36–37, 58–61, 66, 75, 97, 113, 123, 134, 159, 187, 189
ethics, 47, 91, 95, 148, 152, 157, 163, 166, 176, 188–89, 191
  personal, 151, 153, 188
evidence, 66–67, 69–70, 73, 111–12, 182, 184

F

faith
  blind, 5, 65, 82, 98, 109, 111–12, 133, 148, 152, 159, 169–70
  rational, 65–66, 68, 70, 75, 171
fallacies, 76, 184–85

G

globalization, 33
God, v, 4–5, 14, 24, 61, 63–84, 86, 92–93, 98–99, 111–12, 114–16, 163–64, 166–67, 169–71, 178
  existence of, 68, 70, 76–77, 79–80, 169

God-question, 5, 24, 64–66, 70, 76–77, 80–83, 111–12, 178–79, 191
Golden Rule, 91, 157
Gothic cathedral, 51

H

"Harlem" (Hughes), 54–55
Higgs Boson, 73, 97
Hubble Telescope, 79
human nature, 47, 54, 186–87, 190–91

I

ideas
  creative, 160, 184
  intangible, 94–96, 164, 167, 189–90
imagination, 48–49, 51–53, 60, 86, 123, 184, 190
impact, significant, v, 1–2, 6–7, 11, 24, 47, 61, 68–69, 126, 151–53
induction, 68, 127, 136, 182
intangibles, v, 4–5, 10, 12–13, 24, 76, 80–82, 85–87, 90–100, 103–5, 127, 133–35, 137, 150, 178
International Flat Earth Society, 147
interpretations, 48–50, 53, 56, 61, 123
An Introduction to Logic and Scientific Method (Cohen), 7
intuition, 91, 100–102
ISIS (Islamic State of Iraq and Syria) or ISIL, 150
Islam, 5, 64, 83, 150

J

Jews, 65, 129, 172

L

laws, 7, 10, 13, 55, 97, 136–37, 181–82
legacies, 3, 144, 179
life-truths, 20, 54–56
logic, 7, 13, 20, 136–37, 142, 144, 181–85

laws of, 6–7, 9, 13, 20, 92, 127, 133, 136, 181, 183–84
love, 7, 12–14, 21–22, 25, 34, 37, 58, 61, 69, 76, 98, 103–4, 168–69, 173–74, 176–77

M

making meaning, 2–5, 13, 17–19, 21–22, 35–39, 45–47, 59–61, 107–11, 113, 123–24, 143–45, 151–53, 157–59, 163–65, 176–79
  method of, 152–53
Man's Search for Meaning (Frankl), 19
materialism, 10, 43, 66, 80, 85–88, 92, 99, 108–10, 123, 148, 156–59, 170–72, 178
meaning, 1–26, 30–54, 57–61, 63–66, 68–70, 82–84, 86–88, 90–92, 104–5, 107–45, 147–53, 155–61, 163–64, 166–79, 189–92
  absolutes of, 148, 150
  emotional, 57–59
  greatest source of, 64–65, 99
  idea of, 2–4, 10, 15–17, 20, 32, 46–47, 83, 114, 121, 138, 152, 156, 160, 179
  implied, 5, 161, 163, 168–69
  lack of, 18, 42, 104, 141, 159–60
  little, 39, 42, 45, 61, 87
  main sources of, 24, 160
  maker of, 122–23
  objective, 12, 42, 61, 64, 67–69, 72, 75–76, 83, 90, 126–28, 133–35, 147–48, 150–52
  objectivity of, 5, 135, 137
  philosophical, 175
  positive, 116, 140, 142, 150, 153
  sources of, 5, 14, 24–25, 40, 64, 86, 88, 92, 104–5, 113–14, 122, 141, 156, 158–59, 170

subjective, 66, 111, 126–27, 131, 136, 181, 192
meaningfulness, 3, 105, 141, 144, 150–51, 153
Meaning in Life: The Creation of Value (Singer), 176
meaninglessness, v, 3, 5, 8, 11, 78, 104, 116, 127, 140–42, 148, 153, 159
meaning of life, 3, 5, 9–10, 18, 28, 31, 44, 46–47, 52, 61, 86, 156–61, 163, 166–70, 172–79
Meaning of Life, The (Eagleton), 156
Meaning of Life, The (Klemke), 175
Meaning of Life, The (Lichtenbert), 6
meaningology, 4, 16
METHOD of MAKING MEANING, 151–53
Middle Ages, 52, 169
motivation, 37, 110, 112, 192

N

narcissism , 33
New Orleans, 7
nihilism, 5, 79, 127, 140, 142–45, 148, 173
nihilists, 142, 144

O

opinion, 146
opinions, 13, 126, 145–46, 181–83

P

paintings, 51–53, 59–61, 123, 136
philosopher-king, 36
philosophy, 12–13, 17–18, 31, 43, 86, 122, 145, 147–48, 160–61, 163, 166, 168, 178–79, 186–88, 190
personal, 43, 46, 122
physics, 71, 81, 95, 97, 137
current, 97
Plato's philosophy, 36–37, 47

politics, 38, 42, 66, 176
possessions, 86–87, 91, 110, 113, 117, 141, 158–59
pragmatism, 102, 152
premises, 66, 68, 72, 182–85
prescriptions, 4, 12–13, 188
Principia Mathematica (Whitehead and Russell), 136
problems, moral, 152–53, 188–89

R

realities, 5, 12, 90, 112, 166
relationships, 2, 7, 14, 25–28, 30–32, 38, 42, 69, 87, 113, 136, 157, 160, 172, 190–91
relativism, extreme, 5, 127–28, 138, 140, 145–48, 152, 178, 181
relativists, extreme, 134, 145, 147–48

S

Search for Meaning, The (Naylor, Willimon, Naylor), 3–4, 65, 86
seekers, 31–32, 43
subjectivists, 126, 130–31
suicide, 18, 113, 141

T

Taoism, 74
thinking
artistic, 136
creative, 183, 185
critical, 127, 184–85
flesh-and-blood, 28–29
logical, 13, 66, 182
Tikkun magazine, 176
truths, intangible, 54, 81, 83, 90–91, 94–96, 99–100, 102–3, 144, 151, 159
Tulane University, 7
typical people, 38, 110, 129, 148, 168

typical person, 2, 20, 22, 32, 60–61, 110–11, 123, 135, 145–46, 156, 159, 166, 170–71, 178

U

universe, 5, 15, 50, 65, 67–75, 79–80, 82–83, 97, 103, 142, 144, 169
  vastness of, 74, 79–80, 82
utilitarianism, 152

V

values, 5, 10–14, 18, 24–25, 31, 54, 60–61, 69, 99–100, 133–34, 147–48, 152, 166–67, 181, 189–90
voice, inner, 14–15, 93

W

war, 17, 38, 50, 52–53, 66, 74, 76–77, 98–99, 124, 142, 148, 172–74, 183, 187, 189
What Does It All Mean? (Nagel), 3, 176
What's It All About? (Baggini), 176
wisdom, 13, 160
"Written Dialogues" (Lichtenbert), 32

Edwards Brothers Malloy
Thorofare, NJ USA
December 13, 2016